"*Complex Psychological Trauma* is a gift to the reader, whether therapist or client. Dr. Kinsler maps the territory in what is usually a difficult and protracted therapy and highlights the relationship as the most healing dimension, used strategically to counter the shame and mistreatment previously experienced."

Christine A. Courtois, PhD, ABPP, author of
Spiritually Oriented Psychotherapy for Trauma
and *Treating Complex Trauma: A Sequenced,
Relationship-based Approach* (with Julian Ford)

"*Complex Psychological Trauma* is a true gift to the neophyte trauma therapist and to any trauma therapist who was educated primarily in a single paradigm of thought. Readers enter into the experience of Kinsler's highly regarded workshops on the centrality of relationship in healing the traumatized and emerge with a wealth of vicarious experience and practical clinical knowledge sure to enrich their clinical practices."

Richard P. Kluft, MD, PhD, clinical professor of psychiatry,
Temple University School of Medicine, author of
*Shelter from the Storm: Processing the Traumatic Memories of
DID/DDNOS Patients with the Fractionated Abreaction Technique*

"*Complex Psychological Trauma* is both scholarly and practical, a book that integrates theory, process, and the language of psychotherapy for complex trauma. It is a book that belongs on every trauma therapist's bookshelf, one to read and then to return to at the times of impasse and crisis that occur in the work we all do in this field."

Joan A. Turkus, MD, psychiatrist, traumatologist,
psychiatric consultant and cofounder of The Center:
Posttraumatic Disorders Program, Psychiatric Institute of
Washington, DC, and past president of the International
Society for the Study of Trauma and Dissociation

"Philip Kinsler's book is a significant contribution to the field of work that concerns the importance of the relationships between clinicians and those for whom we provide professional services—patients/clients with histories of childhood abuse. This is not only a real contribution to th   ntribution."

D1383232

︙n Frankel, PhD, JD, past president,
︙ternational Society for the Study of
Trauma and Dissociation

COMPLEX PSYCHOLOGICAL TRAUMA

Complex Psychological Trauma takes clinicians beyond the standard approaches for treating simple, single-stressor incident PTSD. Here the focus is on the major choice points that establish the relational conditions for growth and change. In these pages, new and experienced clinicians alike will find specific guidance for acting in a relationally healing manner and refreshingly practical, real-life advice on what to say in challenging therapy situations.

Philip J. Kinsler, PhD, ABPP, is an adjunct associate professor of psychiatry at the Geisel School of Medicine at Dartmouth and instructor of psychiatry at Dartmouth-Hitchcock Medical Center. He is a past president of the International Society for the Study of Trauma and Dissociation and the New Hampshire Psychological Association.

COMPLEX PSYCHOLOGICAL TRAUMA

The Centrality of Relationship

Philip J. Kinsler

Routledge
Taylor & Francis Group

NEW YORK AND LONDON

First published 2018
by Routledge
711 Third Avenue, New York, NY 10017

and by Routledge
2 Park Square, Milton Park, Abingdon, Oxon, OX14 4RN

Routledge is an imprint of the Taylor & Francis Group, an informa business

© 2018 Philip J. Kinsler

The right of Philip J. Kinsler to be identified as author of this work has been asserted by him in accordance with sections 77 and 78 of the Copyright, Designs and Patents Act 1988.

All rights reserved. No part of this book may be reprinted or reproduced or utilised in any form or by any electronic, mechanical, or other means, now known or hereafter invented, including photocopying and recording, or in any information storage or retrieval system, without permission in writing from the publishers.

Trademark notice: Product or corporate names may be trademarks or registered trademarks, and are used only for identification and explanation without intent to infringe.

Library of Congress Cataloging-in-Publication Data
Names: Kinsler, Philip J., author.
Title: Complex psychological trauma : the centrality of relationship / by
    Philip J. Kinsler.
Description: New York, NY : Routledge, 2018. | Includes bibliographical references
    and index.
Identifiers: LCCN 2017015834 (print) | LCCN 2017030944 (ebook) |
    ISBN 9781315651910 (eBook) | ISBN 9781138963153 (hardback) |
    ISBN 9781138963160 (pbk.)
Subjects: LCSH: Psychic trauma—Treatment. | Traumatic psychoses. | Psychotherapy.
Classification: LCC RC552.T7 (ebook) | LCC RC552.T7 K56 2018 (print) |
    DDC 616.85/21—dc23
LC record available at https://lccn.loc.gov/2017015834

ISBN: 978-1-138-96315-3 (hbk)
ISBN: 978-1-138-96316-0 (pbk)
ISBN: 978-1-315-65191-0 (ebk)

Typeset in Caslon Pro
by Apex CoVantage, LLC

To Mugs, my eternal rock

To Heather, Rebecca, Ethan, Ryan, and Connor, who light up my world

Contents

PREFACE

This book is 40 years in the making, from my receipt of relational therapy, to my learning how to practice it with complex trauma survivors, to my abilities to write and present workshops training others. I first published an article describing my views on the work in 1992 (P. J. Kinsler, 1992). At that time, it was outside of the mainstream paradigm. The importance of relational factors has now become common wisdom, and I am gratified by that development.

I have tremendous respect for the shared search for paradigms that work, among the many writers and thinkers and "just regular therapists" who do complex trauma therapy. The blending of technique-based and relational therapies for trauma is in many ways a capstone to my career. In this book, I have tried to present all I have learned about relational factors in therapy for complex trauma survivors. The book is also a plea that we expand our diagnostic working models in an integrationist fashion to develop multi-factorial understandings of our clients.

It is a cliché to thank one's clients; nevertheless I need to offer them deep appreciation. Our clients supervise us. We try something, see how it bounces off this client, reassess. We develop methods that work, through this process of clinical supervision by and through the client's reactions. The complex trauma survivors I have treated have been among the most courageous and persistent human beings I know and I thank them for "training me up."

In developing my thinking regarding relational trauma therapy, I have been supported by truly special colleagues. Dr. Christine Courtois has stood by my side and provided support from the publication of that original paper, through this book. She volunteered her time and expertise to offer a lengthy, learned, and helpful, line by line critique of an earlier version of this work. It is a far better book because of her offering. I have been truly privileged to work closely with Dr. Joan Turkus, who I have previously termed a mentor of mentors. We have thought together, written together, presented together, and developed a deep friendship. Over years of membership and various leadership positions in the International Society for the Study of Trauma and Dissociation, I have worked closely with Dr. Steve Frankel, whose relational understandings are close to my own, and we have joyfully written and presented together. Way back in 1989, Kathy Steele came out with an article called "Sitting with the Shattered Soul" (Steele, 1989) that showed her to be an enormously gifted clinician and member of the relational therapy "tribe." She has gone on to become a senior scholar of this work; we have taught together and workshopped together, and I make a point to attend her trainings because of the depth and heart and quality of her work.

Finally, I want to thank Dr. Richard Kluft. Dr. Kluft took a gamble on an unknown from rural New Hampshire in publishing that original paper. Although he was not in agreement with much of what it said then, he gave it a platform. Now, 25 years later, we are close colleagues. Dr. Kluft stood up for training in complex trauma, the dissociative disorders, and hypnosis under brutal and vicious attack by advocates of the so-called false memory syndrome. He was often alone as their target. Through those experiences he maintained his commitment to scholarship, the preservation of the knowledge of the field, and bringing together analytic, hypnotic, and relational stances to enhance our clinical work.

How does one thank their family for more than 25 years of support? My wife, Margaret "Mugs" Johnston, has been a rock, and in times of discouragement a source of renewed confidence and motivation. My two daughters, Heather Kinsler and Rebecca Malloy, spent much of their childhoods with their father always on call, taking emergency calls when necessary, being drained by the work. They often treated it with acceptance and humor.

One day, I got such an emergency call. My then teenage daughter Heather had apparently listened to many such conversations, despite my taking them in my office and trying to keep them private. After the call, she teased me, saying, "Dad, you should have let me take that one . . . I know that hypnotic intervention you used by heart." It made me think about how much the work had penetrated my family life. I'm quietly pleased that despite their over-exposure in childhood, each of them is pursuing careers centered on psychology, helping, and teaching others. It is all a father could have hoped for.

References

Kinsler, P. J. (1992). The centrality of relationship: What's not being said. *Dissociation: Progress in the Dissociative Disorders, 5*(3), 166–170.

Steele, K. (1989). Sitting with the shattered soul. *Pilgrimage: Journal of Psychotherapy and Personal Exploration, 15*(6), 19–25.

PART I

CORE QUESTIONS AND CONCEPTS

1
INTRODUCTION

This book is written for three purposes. The first is to set the stage, explain basic concepts, and discuss questions the book is meant to answer.

The second is to discuss diagnostic thinking—what concepts are important in trying to understand the client before us? That section of the book presents an integrationist view of diagnosis. Theories are lenses and use of all available lenses, from the biological to the psychosocial, can increase our understanding of clients and improve our abilities to match our techniques to the client.

The third section of the book follows three complex trauma cases through the process of therapy relationship formation, and the actual therapy relationship management work. That section focuses specifically on how to form productive relationships with persons with various experiences of attachment to other human beings. The literature calls these "attachment stances." The book stresses the relationship with the therapist as one of the most central predictors of therapeutic success. I have previously called this "the centrality of relationship" (P. J. Kinsler, 1992, 2014; P. J. Kinsler, Courtois, & Frankel, 2009).

What Is Psychological Trauma?

"Trauma" is a word that has been tossed around so frequently that it bears discussing and defining. There are two approaches to what constitutes a "trauma," the objective and the experiential. A trauma is a psychologically overwhelming experience. It is so overwhelming that typical human information processing is interrupted. This is not the portion of the book to describe that in detail; it is discussed later. But, in brief, let's say something emotional but not overwhelming happens to a person—perhaps we get critical feedback on a paper. Our sense organs perceive what has happened; in this case, we read the feedback, and pass this on to other portions of the brain.

In the most simplistic but useful level of analysis, the brain has three different operations centers. Our so-called reptilian brain, the brain stem, and related organs do things such as regulate our heart rate and breathing automatically so we do not have to consciously think 70 times a minute, "Oh, better contract my heart." In the "critical feedback" example, maybe these portions of our brain up our heart rate and breathing some, because this is what they do when we experience stress.

The second operating system consists of what is called the "limbic system"—those portions of the brain that feel and process fear and other emotions, and that look in our database of prior experience for context. "Hmmm, this is sad and somewhat deflating. Have I seen this before? Where?"

The third operations center is our cortex, which thinks over and makes sense of experience: "Oh, we've gotten this kind of feedback before . . . what did we do? OK, we really did not do our best on that paper . . . something to learn there . . . also, the professor said we did not clearly define certain concepts . . . can go back and look at that. Maybe I didn't get what she/he meant about trauma. I could ask a question in class . . . or I could go and talk to her/him . . . think I'll do that."

A human/interpersonal component is also used to process and resolve the event. This is essentially the question of whether we have been soothed in a way that calms the emotion centers. So, in our poor paper example, we talk to another student. They tell us the professor is a stickler, but one learns from her/him. They know you're smart enough to do a good re-write. They believe in you; they've seen you grow from, and get through, this kind of thing before. As this happens, your breathing starts to slow, your heart rate comes down, likely there's a large, cleansing exhale, you begin to relax and feel OK about yourself again.

What we see here is a process of getting soothed, conceptualizing, making sense of, planning to take control over, and deciding on action steps. This processing has an effect back on the emotion centers. It leads to a felt sense that we have managed the event, come to terms with it; it does not need much further intellectual or emotional work. It feels "resolved" or "mostly resolved."

Psychological trauma interrupts and interferes with these normal stages of event processing. The limbic system goes into fear overdrive. This interferes with connections between the limbic system and the cortex. In effect, our abilities to make sense of, work over, and put away our reactions to the experience are interrupted, and we are left with raw emotion. If there is no soothing, our abilities to calm and re-regulate our physiological reactions are interfered with, as is our sense-making ability. And so, we develop a set of typical reactions to manage this unresolved material (M. Cloitre et al., 2009; van der Kolk, 1996, 2002, 2005, 2014).

These reactions typically come in four areas: intrusive thoughts about the event, efforts to avoid feelings about the event (numbing), hyper-vigilance to stimuli possibly similar to the event (e.g., startle reactions), and changes to our sense of self.

Let's use the "simple" example of a car accident in which your leg is broken but you survive. No one particularly takes care of you. "It's only a broken leg." "Stop making such a big deal." No one soothes the fear, the feeling you might have been killed, the pain of the leg, or the change in your sense of safety. You might then come away with fears of driving, visions of the accident, hyper-anxiety when you attempt to drive, and a permanently changed sense of how safe you are in the world. If you're the self-blaming type—and this book discusses later in considerable detail how this often helps a child process trauma—you might even come away feeling, "I'm an idiot, I should have looked more carefully. I was going 5 mph over the limit. I could have killed someone. I'm a much more awful person than I thought I was before the accident." Thus, we develop all four clusters of what we have come to term posttraumatic stress disorder (PTSD) (American Psychiatric Association, 2000, 2013; van der Kolk, 2014).[1]

What About That Distinction Between Objective and Experiential Trauma?

People react differently to events. Some of this is undoubtedly temperament. Other causes of variability come from whether we have safe and soothing experiences as an infant, and also later in child development (J. Bowlby, 1980, 1983, 1988, 1989; Winnicott, 1958, 1965, 1969). For some persons, relatively mild events from the standpoint of other persons may feel traumatic. For example, it takes the therapist an hour to return an emergency call. Other persons do not experience the emotional overwhelm and frozen fear of trauma despite actual combat experiences.

As a field, we struggle with this phenomenon, and not very well. Our struggles are represented by changes in what we define as Criterion A in our diagnostic manuals for PTSD (American Psychiatric Association, 2000, 2013). We struggle to say what should or should not be considered traumatic. For this book, the content of any particular formation of specific criteria sets is less important than our recognizing the human variability in what feels traumatic, and understanding why, to the person in front of us now, with their history and genetics, the events they are discussing feel like trauma. With certain clients, we, of course, have the task of helping them redefine and re-conceptualize that disappointments or stubbed toes are not typically seen as trauma. But we must also understand how in their inner world, the sense of such events as traumatic came to be. We strive to balance the objective with the phenomenological.

What Is Complex Trauma?

Many persons experience multiple traumas, sometimes over long time periods, and of many different types. It is not unusual for a child to experience physical abuse, neglect, verbal abuse, parental substance abuse and incarceration, and communal/gang violence, over the course of years. This creates the phenomenon of complex trauma, sometimes also called "polyvictimization" (Boxer & Terranova, 2008; Bradley, Jenei, & Westen, 2005; Carlson et al., 2001; C. A. Courtois, 2012; English, Graham, Litrownik, Everson, & Bangdiwala, 2005; D. Finkelhor, Ormrod, & Turner, 2007; D. Finkelhor, Ormrod, Turner, & Hamby, 2005;

Ford, Elhai, Connor, & Frueh, 2010; Ford, Grasso, Hawke, & Chapman, 2013; Hamby, Finkelhor, Turner, & Ormrod, 2010; Herrenkohl & Herrenkohl, 2007; Higgins & McCabe, 2001; Holt, Finkelhor, & Kantor, 2007; Renner & Slack, 2006; Smith, McCart, & Saunders, 2008; Turner, Finkelhor, Hamby, & Shattuck, 2013; Turner, Finkelhor, & Ormrod, 2010; van der Kolk, 2007).

How Is Complex Trauma Different From Single-Event Trauma?

The more types of trauma a person experiences, the greater the effect on the survivor. A dose-response relationship exists between the number and variety of types of trauma experienced, and later psychological and physiological/health effects. (Felitti, 1998) Trauma over the course of a childhood affects the growing child's entire sense of him/herself, and of the world around them. "Are people safe? Am I worth loving? Can I ever relax without danger sneaking up on me? I must have brought this on. If only I were better this would not happen. I better learn how to please the people abusing me. Close feelings only result in abuse and rape."

Human beings are sense-makers. We try to find a way to make sense of the world and ourselves, even in the face of the worst horror (Frankl, 1997). Complex trauma affects everything: how we think, how we feel, how we relate to others, how we relate to ourselves.

Complex trauma also affects physiological unfolding and development (Figueroa & Silk, 1997; Porges, 2001; A. N. Schore, 1994, 1996, 1997, 1998a, 1998b, 2000a, 2000b, 2001a; Strathearn, 2007). This topic, often called *epigenetics*, occupies entire volumes of learned literature. For this book, it is enough to say that complex abuse experiences influence the physiological development of brain systems involved in threat evaluation, sense of self, establishment and maintenance of social and love relationships, and regulation of upset—our entire emotion regulation system. Effects of complex trauma are substantial and global across child development.

Although researchers have often focused on one or another type of victimization—physical abuse, exposure to domestic violence, sexual abuse, etc—the natural history of our clients shows exposures to many types of violence/abuse within their families. A study published in June 2015, as this book was being written, used data from the National Survey of Children's Exposure to Violence. Results showed that:

> It was common for children and youth to be exposed to multiple types of episodes over the course of a year. In total, 40.9% had more than 1 direct experience of violence, crime, or abuse, 10.1% had 6 or more, and 1.2% had 10 or more. Overall, 60.8% of the children had at least 1 form of direct exposure in the last year. When witnessing and indirect exposures were combined with direct exposure, 67.5% of the children had at least 1 exposure, 50% had more than 1 exposure, 15.0% had 6 or more exposures, and 4.4% had 10 or more exposures.

Furthermore:

> . . . experiencing one type increased the likelihood of experiencing other types as well. For example, having a past year physical assault was associated with a 4.9 times higher likelihood of experiencing a sexual offense and a 3.4 times higher likelihood of caregiver maltreatment . . . every combination had a significant risk amplification.
>
> (D. Finkelhor, Turner, Shattuck, & Hamby, 2015)

Not quite tongue in cheek, I have previously written that the clients who come for long-term trauma therapy are survivors of "horrible life disorder" (P. J. Kinsler & Saxman, 2007). For some reason, I've had trouble getting this into the *DSM*.

The data above are not from clinical cases, but from a *national epidemiological sample*. And *20% of non-clinically selected children experience multiple types of victimization over a single calendar year!* Lives such as these predispose to physical health (Felitti, 1998) and general psychiatric issues, depression, substance abuse, and juvenile justice involvement (Elhai et al., 2012; Ford et al., 2010; Spinazzola et al., 2005).

Do We Need Special Methods to Treat Complex Trauma?

Perhaps there are clinicians who can effectively deal with complex trauma using only manualized therapies and exposure treatments. This book will not resolve those arguments. My experiences, and those of multitudes of therapists and clients, show that very often much more is needed. As I and other highly valued colleagues have stated before:

> Child abuse and attachment failures are relational events and experiences, occurring most often within families, between parents and children. The consequences profoundly affect the child's physiological/biological and psychological development, and ability to form close and trusting relationships. Victimized children are hurt in relationships, yet, paradoxically, *relationships can be the core component of healing from these injuries.* At times, special relationships such as close friendships, mentorships, marriages, partnerships and, in some cases, parenting of one's own children, can be restorative when they provide the attachment security the individual needs to learn new ways of relating [to] and trusting others. Psychotherapy may also provide the needed "safe haven" within which to modify old relational patterns that were built on insecurity and exploitation. Stated simply, whether it occurs within or outside of psychotherapy, healing of complex and chronic trauma associated with abuse (especially when there is a foundation of attachment trauma) occurs in safe, dependable, kind, and bounded relationships.
>
> (P. J. Kinsler et al., 2009, p. 183)

What Are These Attachment Stances Anyway? Why Are They Important?

Attachment theory is presented in far greater detail later. For those without a basic introduction, let's start out with the fact that the human infant is entirely dependent on others for safety and survival at birth, and for very lengthy times thereafter. And never forget that infants have global/whole person experiences (Main, Kaplan, & Cassidy, 1985). Who has not experienced a fussy infant going instantly to joy when cuddled right, or distracted by a toy, or tossed in the air and caught by grandpa or grandma? Infants depend on adults for soothing and safety, which they are not developmentally or physically capable of providing for themselves. When the infant-to-toddler is effectively responded to often enough when they are emotionally dysregulated—when they experience "good enough mothering"—they develop an internal felt sense that they are safe in the world, and that there are secure and dependable sources of calming out there (J. Bowlby, 1988; Main, 1995, 2000; Main, Hesse, & Kaplan, 2005; Winnicott, 1957a, 1957b, 1958). We call this *secure attachment*. It produces children with the general sense that the environment is primarily trustable and that they are also people worthy of care and safety.

What if the relationships are not so safe, stable, and predictable? There are then three main ways of forming an overarching sense (schema) about self and world. Two kinds of insecure attachments can form. In one case, the baby/toddler experiences inconsistent soothing and becomes ambivalent; they want and need safety and contact, but are afraid it will be taken away. So, they fearfully cling. This is called *insecure/ambivalent*, or, in some writings, *insecure/preoccupied*. The child is clingy and preoccupied with the fear of loss. Strike any parallels with many clients' dependent behaviors?

Other children may yearn for connection, but firmly believe it will never be out there. So, they develop armor. "I don't need anything, I won't lean on anyone; you can't hurt me if I don't let you in." The fancy term for this is *insecure/resistant*. Sometimes, our adult "over-functioners" come from this stance. Other times, just our social isolates.

Finally, what if nothing the child does leads to any predictable reaction from the caretakers? One minute safety; another horrid abuse; a third, shame-filled apologies, yet another, physical attack. Nowhere to turn. No home base. No safety. Danger all around. A risk of overwhelming anxiety all around. The feeling of an encroaching bottomless black pit. These are our chaotic attachment clients, and many such clients are found among our complex trauma and dissociative patients.

A basic tenet of this book is that complex psychological trauma therapy seeks to heal and change these core difficult attachment patterns to more stable, safe, predictable ones. And, that as the wounds are primarily relational, so are many of the healing processes.

This is a book about helping to get persons from the various harmful attachment stances to "earned security" through the provision of safe relational therapy.

So, What Is "Earned Secure" Attachment Anyway?

Complex trauma therapy that seeks to change the client's entire inner sense of self/world targets the eventual development of earned security. A core tenet is to give the client a relationship that is different from what they grew up in. So, if we are dependable in the face of chaos; if we are non-blaming and kind, but firm, towards dependency needs; if we apply only the tolerable amount of heat to the armor until it gradually begins to melt; then the experiences in the therapy relationship are taken in. They become a felt antidote to the prior experiences, expectations, and assumptions about life.

"Wait a minute, all those times I called therapist X when I was frightened, they were kind. But they also protected themselves from my calling endlessly; they helped me believe I could manage more myself, but also that there was a person there for me. Maybe I really am worth something and maybe all of life is not deprivation and rejection." As the inner felt sense changes, so does how they put themselves across to others in their environment. They get different reactions, they are not instantly rejected as "too needy," and their life gets better. They have at least begun the path to earned security.

Why Focus on Relationships?

Some of this was discussed previously. A different relationship with a therapist is a change agent. There are also practical reasons. Although the results of therapy outcome research vary somewhat, the core findings are that therapy outcome in general depends most on a few things. The most important of these is the motivation of the client. The second most important is the relationship with the therapist. Specific techniques employed account for far less of the outcome than motivation and relationship. And, a good and safe therapy relationship can also increase client motivation. The therapy relationship is a central and major source of the effect therapy can have. We'll return to this in detail later. A vast research base supporting the importance of the therapy relationship in both general and trauma therapy exists (Bergin & Strupp, 1970; Bohart & Tallman, 2010; Campbell, Norcross, Vasquez, & Kaslow, 2013; Carkhuff & Truax, 1966; C. A. Courtois & Ford, 2013; C. J. Dalenberg, 2004; Duncan, 2010; Gelso, 2009a, 2009b).

How Was the Six Crises Model Developed? Is There Any Validation?

A consensus of complex trauma thinkers and therapists describe a three-stage model of complex trauma therapy. First, there is a period of stabilization and teaching of resources/ways to manage memories and emotional storms. Then there is a period of processing traumatic material, so-called working through, generally following the model of information processing described previously. Finally, there is a period of expansion of the client's life and re-connection to the world outside (M. Cloitre et al., 2011; C. A. Courtois, 2004, 2010; C. A. Courtois & Ford, 2013; J. Herman, 2015; Judith Lewis Herman, 1992; Judith L. Herman, 2012; Janoff-Bulman & McPherson Frantz, 1997; P. J. Kinsler, 2014; Pearlman, 1997).

I have had the privilege and mystery of working with complex trauma survivors for more than 40 years, and have had the warm colleagueship of many of the thinkers and healers previously referenced. In these years of work, and theorizing/exploring with colleagues, regular patterns have emerged. The therapist always needs to form a directed relationship or one happens by default. Clients routinely test us in emergent situations. Hurt and pain and rage hit when one processes trauma. All things going at least somewhat according to plan, a mutual termination occurs and must be dealt with. Or, there is a premature termination for many reasons.

The six crises described in this book are based essentially on narrative theory. What commonalities can be gleaned from all this data? What are the themes? The crises are from the realm of personal experience, and the shared experience from many colleagues. The validation at present is the generally favorable and enthusiastic reception from both experts and newbies to complex trauma therapy who find that the crises make sense, they validate their experiences, they provide some guidance in how to maneuver over time in the therapy. I hope that readers find the work similarly helpful.

What Do These Odd Terms Mean and How Are They Important?

Every field has specialized vocabulary. I seek to write as clearly and simply as possible, and to refine concepts to their core meaning. It has been said that there are two types of thinkers: lumpers and splitters. Lumpers look for the commonalities, the core. Splitters attend to the differences. I am an unabashed lumper, a synthesizer. Even so, I sometimes discuss words that are bandied about in the trauma field that readers of this book, particularly students/residents in early training, will not have heard. In general, terms are defined as they are presented. Where further explanation seems useful, they are footnoted.

Now, before we turn to the delivery and management of relational therapy for complex trauma, let's look more deeply at how we think about and understand patients.

Note

1. This is a very basic schematic outline. For a much more thorough discussion, read further in the book to the relevant chapters, and consult the van der Kolk and *DSM* materials referenced previously.

PART II
THEORETICAL LENSES

2
THE THERAPIST'S THINKING TASKS

Human behavior is a river with many tributaries. Unfortunately, most psychological theories of understanding human behavior focus on one tributary and leave out the others. The theorists then develop a model of therapeutic change based on that singular focus. And then they argue why that tributary is the best and only one. This is not helpful for the working therapist or the therapist in training. Therapists come out "an inch wide and a mile deep," being deeply inculcated in one model and unaware of, or unable to fully comprehend and use, the others.

How then should a complex trauma therapist think? What variables are important? What change methods? What theoretical perspectives help or hurt?

Let's go a little more deeply into the common experiences of our complex trauma clients. Complex trauma survivors are abused and otherwise subjected to violence and mistreatment within family or communal contexts, in multiple ways, across significant lengths of time. They experience combinations of physical abuse, sexual abuse, parental substance abuse, neglect, verbal abuse, communal lack of safety, and/or parental incarceration. Multiple changes of caretakers, schools, and residences occur often. Many experience the instability of the foster care/ juvenile residential placement systems. The more types of abuse they suffer, in general, the greater are the psychological and physiological consequences (Boxer & Terranova, 2008; Carlson et al., 2001; Donovan, 1991; English et al., 2005; Felittih, 1998; D. Finkelhor, Ormrod, & Turner, 2007; Ford, Elhai, Connor, & Frueh, 2010).

Yet, not every victim responds in the same way. Some seem crushed, others remarkably resilient. We cannot assume we know the effects of a traumatic upbringing on a client. We need to develop a working theory *about this client, with these experiences, now, as they sit with me.*

Throughout this book, I tell stories, often of my mistakes and what I've learned from them. So, here's an example of mucking up a therapy by making untested assumptions about the meanings a client made of her traumas:

> It must have been a lazy day. We all have them, though we are, of course, loath to admit it to ourselves. I was spending the day muttering supportive inanities rather than listening. A client told me of her years of sexual abuse at the hands of a violent, alcoholic, "backwoods like from the movie Deliverance" father. I had let such stories become old hat. I muttered, "Oh, that must have been horrible for you," thinking I was providing empathy. She bolted upright in her chair, laughed, flung out her hands in an open gesture and said, "Are you kidding? I loved it! It was the only time he wasn't beating the shit out of me!" Once again, I re-learned about listening for the meaning *particular to* this client.

So, for each client, we must create and test a matrix of propositions that help us understand this individual person—sets of hypotheses to understand their inner worlds. Of course, our generating these hypotheses depends on the many different "thinking and feeling tests" we silently propose to our minds and our hearts in trying to fashion "a theory of this person." And we are guided by what has come before us, by what our theories have trained us to pay attention to.

As we sit in the therapy room, what *should* we think about? What are the threads for constructing this "tapestry of the client"?

Therapy is a process of monitoring multiple levels of interaction and deciding which to respond to, if any. Following are some of the things one might/should think about during the session:

1. The *content* of what the client is saying. It is always a good idea to pay attention to the current struggles and events reported. Therapists must keep the content continually in mind, while exploring other levels. There are many other levels:

2. *How* is the client saying what he/she is saying? What is the emotional tone? Are they flat and turned off and numbed out? Approaching emotional overload and dysregulation? Are they unconsciously looking to pull certain responses from the therapist?

3. What am I as the *therapist feeling?*
   a. How much of this is my issue vs. important information about the client's interpersonal operations?

4. What is the *client feeling?*
   a. Are they aware of these feelings?
   b. Suppressing them?
   c. Exaggerating them?
   d. Performing because of what they think the therapist expects?

5. Is this behavior a *re-enactment* of a familiar prior scene? Does the client know this?

6. How is the *client perceiving* me?
   a. What of this is true about me, fortunately or unfortunately?
   b. What of this is the client's projection?
   c. And where does that projection come from anyway?
   d. And if it's accurate about me, do I need supervision or consultation or therapy to work on that?

7. How am I *perceiving the client?*
   a. What of this is accurate?
   b. What of this is my own stuff?
   c. What of this is quick diagnostic stereotyping?
   d. What of this is accurate and may guide the work?

8. How are we *relating?* Is this relationship being experienced as helpful, harmful, neutral, frightening, healing at this moment?

9. Am I noticing any patterns in what the client describes? Are the ways they are acting now, with me, characteristic of them? If so, what kinds of interpersonal reactions might they typically draw from others?

10. Is this a time to *respond or just listen*? How do I judge this?
11. And, finally, *what if anything do I say*?

The mental process of the therapist is akin to the vaudeville performer spinning multiple plates on sticks and trying to keep them all from crashing. Or of the visit to the optometrist, where a different lens clicks in and makes the stimulus clearer or blurrier. And all of this is going on in the blink of a second or two, before the therapist decides whether, and how to, respond.

Theories are how we make sense of these multiple-level transactions, and how we decide on what's next. Let's look at the contributions of various theories to what we think about and do in treatment, when confronted with the confusing matrix of thought processes just discussed.

3

CONTRIBUTIONS OF THE LESS
TRAUMA-AWARE SCHOOLS
OF THERAPY

In building our "theory of the client" it's important to think from multiple perspectives and to find the contributions we can use to grind our glasses to the correct prescription for this client. Rather than one theory explaining all, we look through multiple lenses and use the understandings of different theories as necessary. We click the theoretical lenses into the optometrist-like device of our theory-building mind, and use the input from those lenses in clarifying the current issues. We are "mental psychotherapy integrationists."

Let's look at the contributions offered us by some of the major schools of psychopathology and psychotherapy.[1]

Psychoanalytic Theory

Because many therapists are no longer trained in analytic-based models, it is important to review the core conceptions of this model to expand the possible base of responses available to the therapist.

The Conflict Model

Being traumatized doesn't account for everything. Sometimes, it's just "regular stuff." The basic tenet of psychoanalysis surrounding symptom formation is that symptoms arise because of internal conflicts between our impulses/feelings and the prohibitions we've learned in childhood, the taboos. It's a hydraulic model. Translated into somewhat more modern language, our needs, wants, and impulses exert pressure towards expression. Childhood teaches us which of those are acceptable and not acceptable; we form a 'superego.' It's the part of the mind that says "No, better not . . ." The ego tries to resolve the two pressures, channeling the "steam" of the impulses/needs/feelings into acceptable outlets. In a well-functioning person, the hydraulics work—the impulses are channeled into acceptable expression. In a troubled person, the pipes burst and the symptoms spray out.

The core of the model involves thinking a person's psychology is like the workings of a steamship. No coincidence that these were the height of technology as Freud created his thinking.

Your *id*, which is actually translated from the German as the *it* or the *essence*, is the fire burning in your boiler—impulses, wishes, desires. For Freud, these were sex and aggression.

All that fire produces a lot of steam, which can't be allowed to just explode. Your *superego* (again, from the German, the "over-I") contains the regulations and prohibitions about how and where the steam may be used.

Your *ego*, your "I" from the German, essentially is a set of valves that determine how the steam can be diverted and expressed in socially acceptable ways:

> Your ego functions as essentially a bunch of valve adjusters. It channels the energy/steam into socially acceptable functioning.

Symptoms are a failure of the valve adjusters to work right, producing either too much inhibition or too little:

> To continue this over-wrought metaphor to its well-deserved death, you get symptoms of "the constipated id": depression, somatization, schizoid withdrawals, flattened affect. You get disorders of "the explosive id": antisocial behavior, sexual acting out, impulse control disorders, and possibly grandiosity. You get symptoms of "the id-superego war": essentially the anxiety disorders and obsessions and compulsions.

Now, this is a bit tongue in cheek, but in truth, much clinical thinking sticks right with this metaphor. For years, it was a meme, if you will, of psychoanalytic training to say that "to treat an obsessive you have to teach him/her to feel (more id); to teach a hysteric (*histrionic* in our current terms), you need to teach him/her to think." Hydraulic thinking, I say.

To go on with more useful parts of the model:

> Different families create different (or sometimes unfortunately no) prohibitions on impulse/feeling expression. Societies create child-rearing practices to inculcate that society's taboos and create the kinds of adults that society needs (Erikson, 1950; Erikson, 1980). All these processes go on in addition to traumatic experiences. You get "trauma plus."

In prototypical Western culture, there are certain common taboos. These often include anger, sexuality, dependency, sadness and hurt, self-assertion, and accomplishment. You can probably create your own list. The point is that trauma survivors have the very same internal conflicts as everyone else, and we need to look at their behaviors inside and outside the therapy relationship as reflections of their familial and societal conflicts as well as their traumas.

The Developmental Model

Psychoanalysis offers us the idea of stages in the life cycle where certain conflicts and themes are central. Major developmental tasks occur in a typical pattern. Although we certainly may argue about the proper names, and the pattern of unfolding of these stages, it remains clinically useful to ask ourselves what developmental stage-specific struggle might be occurring for the client in front of us. We want to look at what this client learned about basic safety; about their dependency/attachment needs; about the possibility of a sense of autonomy rather than being continually plagued by shame and doubt (Erikson, 1950). What did they learn about their growing self-assertion and abilities? About their expressions of tenderness or anger? About demonstrating or not demonstrating achievements? About whether it is OK to separate from and leave the parents or not? As we flip through our mental notecards about stages of human development, we continue to build our internal working model of this client.

Transference and Countertransference

From the perspective of 50 years in the field, it seems unbelievable and perhaps insulting to the reader to have to review the basic insights surrounding transference and countertransference. However, in many cases this is not being taught, given the academic pressures for teaching only "evidence-based treatments." Let me once again remind readers that "good old-fashioned psychotherapy" has been known to be an effective evidence-based treatment since the 1970s:

> Here's what can happen when these ideas are not taught. I was once a member of my state licensing board. We received a complaint. A client accused their therapist of abandonment. The client had gone to a community clinic for help with depression. The clinician had been trained only in manualized therapies. The therapist offered the client six or eight sessions to work through a depression treatment manual. The client agreed. During the manualized treatment, the client began to develop feelings of attachment towards the therapist. The client felt understood, cared for, listened to. At the end of the manual, the client requested further treatment. The therapist demurred, saying that the treatment had been completed according to the book. The client felt abandoned and hurt enough that he/she filed a complaint. The therapist had to respond, first in writing and then in person. The therapist's defense? "Transference feelings do not develop during cognitive-behavioral manualized treatment for depression." Funny thing, both the evidence in front of the clinician, and in front of the board, showed differently. The board felt the clinician needed further training and prescribed a re-education plan to broaden the therapist's understanding of therapist-client interactions.

The central theoretical idea around transference of use to trauma therapists is that we all live in a movie of our own creation. It is as if we have a video projector in our foreheads and that projector sends out a movie composed of all our prior important interpersonal learning, and we then live as if that movie was "the truth," "reality."

When I teach workshops, I use the following story to illustrate this point:

> I was leaving for a conference. Right before I left, a referral of a new client came in to my answering machine. I was essentially "out the door," late for a plane, and could not respond. At the airport, I changed my answering machine message to say I was away at a conference and that all calls would be returned after that conference. I left instructions about the coverage I had arranged for emergencies while I was gone. I had never met the person who called and had no treatment contract or responsibilities. I left a clear message about when non-emergent calls would be returned.
>
> When I got back from the conference, there were a series of messages on my answering machine from this unknown person. The first of these went something like: "So I'm not even important enough to return my call before you leave, huh!" A message a few hours later said, "Boy, you must be a narcissistic son of a bitch; have to announce you're away at a conference!" A day or so later there was another message: "Apparently, you don't care about anyone but yourself! It's two days and you haven't returned my call!" And finally, several hours after that: "You miserable bastard, I don't want therapy from you after all; who do you think you are!"

My "stimulus input" to this series of transactions was very minimal. I had no personal contact at all. The person responded completely to what his/her projections, his/her transferred attitudes, made of my phone messages. In his/her personal movie, these routine answering machine contacts signaled deep interpersonal rejection and lack of caring, with almost no input from me. My answering machine became a projection screen for the potential client's internal worldview.

We need to understand the movies clients make about us, and about other important people in their lives. We also need to monitor our own movies as we react to our clients, to separate what of their reactions is due to their moviemaking, and what is due to their correct perceptions of us, about our own unresolved struggles. Thus, we must be sensitive to and monitor *countertransference*:

> An embarrassing but true personal story: It was a very cold winter's Saturday in New Hampshire. I had a day's worth of work to grade student papers. I got up early to ensconce myself in our family room with a cozy wood fire. I asked my wife not to interrupt me; I had lots of work to do. She said, "Fine, we are leaving for dinner at the Smiths at 6:30. Before we go, could you get the mail and move your shoes off the stairs?" (Insert any two minor stupid household requests taking less time to do than to write about.) I said "Sure." Fast forward about 12 hours, with absolutely no interaction. My wife tentatively sticks her head in the family room and says, "Honey, we have to leave in fifteen minutes. Did you happen to get the mail and move your shoes?" To which I responded from my finest well-analyzed, multiple years in therapy self: "You get the hell off my back and stop telling me what to do all the time!" For some unknown reason, we rode in stony silence towards our dinner engagement. As I recall, my wife was driving with her head rigidly forward, no peripheral glances at me, tensed shoulders and tight mouth, for maybe 10 miles. Finally, she looked at me and very firmly and distinctly enunciated, said: "Where . . . does . . . two . . . sentences . . . in twelve . . . hours . . . come out . . . as *always bossing you around and telling you what to do*!?" I gulped and said, "Oh, you think it's my mother stuff?" We both laughed hysterically and went on to a nice dinner.
>
> The trauma therapist has a responsibility to monitor how his/ her own unresolved material may leak into the room. It's not always the client's stuff.

The Radical Notion of a Talking Cure

Psychoanalysis reminds us that the talking and relating cure is a way forward for trauma survivors and others in need of help. As Horvath and Luborsky said, ". . . the ability of the intact portion of the client's conscious, reality-based self to develop a covenant with the 'real' therapist makes it possible to undertake the task of healing" (Horvath & Luborsky, 1993, p. 561).

Ego and/or Self-Psychology Theories

One of the major dissatisfactions with classic Freudian theory was that it seemed to have no place for positive motivations towards learning and mastery so clearly shown in actual observation of children. Could all behavior be reduced to sex and aggression? Weren't there any positive motivations or drives? These dissatisfactions led to the development of theories postulating that the ego or later, the self, developed with independent drives for mastery. Observe a baby try to crawl or walk or say his or her first words and it is hard to deny an independent push to competence. One of the seminal papers in this development was by Robert W. White called "Motivation reconsidered: The concept of competence" (1959). White said:

> Theories of motivation built upon primary drives cannot account for playful and exploratory behavior. The new motivational concept of "competence" is introduced, indicating the biological significance of such behavior. It furthers the learning process of effective interaction with the environment. While the purpose is not known to animal or child, an intrinsic need to deal with the environment seems to exist and satisfaction ("the feeling of efficacy") is derived from it.
>
> (p. 297)

As trauma therapists, one important lens then becomes how were the child's pushes for independent competence handled?

Heinz Kohut and colleagues thought and wrote incisively about major functions parents perform as children develop. Kohut asked whether two major parental functions had been met: *mirroring* and *idealizing* (Kohut, 1977; Kohut & Wolf, 1992). For Kohut, mirroring meant the parent's admiration of the child's possibilities and encouragement thereof. Idealizing meant the parent being a model of what it was to be an admirable human being. Failure of mirroring could lead to an overburdened personality, tormented by feelings of inadequacy. Lack of models could lead to emptiness, lack of direction, lack of motivation, and failure to form a firm personal identity (Kohut & Wolf, 1992).

The ego psychologists provide several additional lenses to our conceptualization of complex trauma clients:

1. What was done in this client's upbringing about their independent explorations and desire for mastery?
2. Were these clients, as children, admired for who they could become or left either empty or overburdened by doubt?
3. Did parents provide positive models of what it meant to be a successful human being? If not, what were the models they did provide of how to be a grown-up adult?

The foregoing discussion describing classic psychoanalysis and its expansion into ego psychology and self-psychology realms is accurate as a description of the original models and their relations to psychological trauma. It is also important to note that as the pervasiveness of childhood trauma in our culture has become far better known over the past 15 to 20 years, some analytic writers have developed more trauma-aware thinking within psychoanalysis. Readers are referred specifically to the works of Philip Bromberg and of Elizabeth Howell (Bromberg, 2003, 2006, 2008, 2009, 2013, 2014, 2016; Howell, 2011).

Behavioral Theory

The intent of this chapter is not to give working therapists an expansive cookbook of every contribution of every major theory. Therapists should/do perform constant hypothesis generation as they listen. "Could it be this? Might that concept explain the generation of this client's behavior? How do I understand and/or intervene?" This chapter reviews major constructs so that we may quickly test out ideas generated by numbers of theories in our moment-to-moment work with clients. Extensive practical and theoretical works on the use of behavioral models in trauma therapy exist (Foa, 2009; Hembree & Foa, 2010; McLean, Asnaani, & Foa, 2015; Nayak, Powers, & Foa, 2012). Readers who desire an extensive background in behavioral methods are referred to the works just referenced. The following section reviews basic tenets of behavioral theory that can be useful to the working trauma clinician.

For this chapter, I divide strictly behavioral contributions from cognitive-behavioral ones.

Skinner taught us that with proper rewards and punishments, one could teach a pigeon to play ping-pong (Epstein, Lanza, & Skinner, 1981; Ferster & Skinner, 1957a, 1957b; Skinner, 1992). Human behavior can be produced by what families reinforce, punish, or ignore. *It is a useful empirical concept to keep asking the question in one's own mind: "What did the family have to act like to produce/reinforce this behavior?"*

Skinner also taught us that certain reinforcement patterns are very difficult to extinguish. Behaviors that are reinforced positively about a third of the time become powerfully "locked in" (Ferster & Skinner, 1957b). Understanding the power of this pattern of intermittent reinforcement helps comprehend when our clients repeatedly reach out for affection from partners who combine extensive abuse with occasional expressions of love. Understanding this pattern helps produce patience in dealing with the many times that domestic violence survivors return to the very persons who injure them most. As multiple clients have said, "The making up is so sweet." It takes a lot of patience and reinforcement of *different* behaviors to help break these patterns. *Often the therapy relationship is the paradigm of a relationship that can be kind and supportive and caring without abuse.*

Social Learning Theory

How do children learn to be a mother, a father, a worker, a partner? Although there are depictions on the internet and/or in media, videogames, schooling, grandparents, and other sources, our parents are our primary models of what it is like to be human. We imitate them continually (Bandura & Barab, 1971; Bandura, Ross, & Ross, 1963; Bandura & Walters, 1963). Years later, we find ourselves saying phrases to our own children we swore would never come out of our mouths. As we age, we recognize that much of who we are comes from our parents, despite our best efforts to leave behind their difficulties, which were *so* apparent to us in adolescence. As the famous philosopher Paul Simon was known to sing, "After changes upon changes we are more or less the same." As you ask your clients to describe their parents in detail, whether in initial history-taking or as therapy progresses, *listen for the basic lessons that the parents modeled.* Our children learn from *how we are*, more than from what we say. Therapeutically, *ask what models did this client's parents present about what it meant to be a grown-up?*

> I was on a car ride with my very hard-working, driven father years ago just after his retirement. He spoke about how he thought he might never be able to slow down, to stop the spinning in his head, the drive to accomplish things; he might never learn to go slowly. I resented much of that as a child. Now I sit here as a 70-year-old man who still works, and writes a book, and heads trauma organizations, and does major criminal forensic cases. Learning by imitation, I say.

The Cognitive-Behavioral Paradigm

Readers may be very familiar with cognitive-behavioral thinking, as it is now widely taught in graduate training. Yet it is a perspective that not everyone knows or uses. Therapists trained in mainly dynamic models may miss the usefulness of this paradigm as they think about clients. The paradigm is useful in both creating a theory of the client and a model of change. For decades, psychology has debated whether emotional experiences are the "primary" causes of our actions, or whether our thoughts and cognitions lead the way (Lazarus, 1984; Rachman, 1981; Zajonc, 1984). For the complex trauma therapist, it turns out this is a both-and. Intense emotions can overwhelm thinking capacity as seen in flashbacks, disorientation from the present, dissociation.

However, the thinking portion of the brain also prompts and helps manage the emotional centers. What we think influences what the emotion centers of the brain will "pass up" to the cortex and view as primary and important. It sets the "filters" of the emotion and attention system. A combat veteran may have a completely different set of filters and assumptions about the meaning of a firecracker than a joyous child.

Cognitive-behavioral theorizing and treatment work on the thought patterns that establish our filters and our interpretation of those firecrackers. Thought exercises, skills training, and increasing levels of exposure to traumatic material, while the client is relaxed, are used to change the perceptions of events previously connected to trauma.

These methods may work completely for some clients, and partially for others. Working therapists try to determine under what circumstances they are useful. For whom? When? In what kinds of settings?

For significant numbers of trauma patients I have treated over the years, the exercises and homework of cognitive-behavioral therapy have been adjunctive aids in managing symptoms, while more relationship-based treatment has reduced the necessity of such symptoms. The cognitive-behavioral work has been the equivalent of developing and managing a better exhaust valve for the pressure cooker, while the relationship-based trauma therapy has turned down the flame, producing the pressure that the valve needs to manage. Other therapists claim success taking a totally cognitive-behavioral approach towards complex trauma. This has not been my experience.

Systems Theories

The central insight of systems theories is that *the whole is more than the sum of its parts* (Von Bertalanffy, 1952). If we take a spark plug out of its engine and look at it, we see some metal and some ceramics; maybe we even can identify that the bottom looks like an electrode. We don't know what it does or how it functions in the engine though, until we look at it in the context of that engine. Only then can we see that it gets electrical impulses, makes a spark, lights up the gasoline, and causes an explosion in the cylinder. And then we can step back and see that the cylinder goes up and down as the pulsed explosions happen. And when we back up farther, we can see that the cylinder is connected to a shaft and that shaft rotates as the cylinder goes up and down, and later that shaft makes the transmission turn, and that eventually makes the wheels turn. The function of the spark plug in the system is what's important.

Von Bertalanffy (1952) and others noted that human beings play a spark plug–like role in family and social systems. Although an individual person has her/his characteristics, he/she also play roles within the family, and the family exerts pressure to perform and to stay in those roles.

Ever go to your parents' home for a holiday and feel the pressures there to act in ways that feel old, but you're pushed there as if by some invisible force? Find yourself playing the good son, the rebel, the dutiful daughter, the caretaker of Mom or Dad? *Systems theory offers trauma therapists a lens to look at the functional roles our clients enact within families.* How do the behaviors and interactions we see within the therapy mirror the roles clients learned within their home environments? What are the pressures to stay in role? What are the possible losses from leaving those well-oiled roles? What might happen to the larger familial context were our client to change? As we listen to our clients tell their trauma stories, we also need to listen for how these traumatic events played into the family system. Did the client's taking a beating prevent Mom from getting one? Did having sex with brother keep him from hurting someone else? Did never asserting one's rights prevent Father from exploding? Did not complaining about Mom or Dad's drug or alcohol use preserve shaky family unity?

As we listen, we place our client's traumatic experiences within the context in which they were created. The therapist can then understand their functions, and can create therapeutic foci and emphases. We can help our clients achieve freedom from these unconsciously powerful familial pressures.

We may also be able to intervene on the family level in ways that free our clients from these role expectations. If we can perhaps help Daddy be less threatened by our client's success, for example, we can free that client to achieve.

Socio-Cultural Theories

If we look at our clients' behaviors through the wrong end of the binoculars, and get some distanced viewing of them, we can see the influence of culture and subculture on the client before us. We learn to ask culturally embedded questions: What was the meaning of respect within this ethnicity and/or subculture? The role of women? The role of men? How does this culture or subculture view individuality vs. familial or cultural cohesion? What role does religion and/or spirituality play in this client's upbringing? In their current struggles? In how they conceptualize good or bad relationships? How does the general organization of the society this client came from influence who he/she is before you? If he/she recently emerged from a different culture, what cultural conflicts may be occurring in his/her life?

What relationship do poverty, community chaos, discrimination, and sexual-orientation status and struggles have to this client's struggles? Has the client ever even felt the right to question cultural assumptions and imperatives? How unsettling is this? And finally, how does this society conceptualize a "proper" adult identity, and how does the society go about producing the kinds of adults it needs through the child-rearing and educational practices adopted (Erikson, 1950; Erikson, 1962; Erikson, 1975)?

It is a bit like peeling an onion. There are many layers. While listening, the therapist's mind is also sorting, scanning the layers, trying to determine what fits. What may be useful in understanding here? What may be useful in forming an intervention? In managing the relationship with this client?

As we rapidly sort in our mind's eye, lines of causality surrounding this client's struggles will become apparent and illuminating, in addition to the trauma perspective. Our clients are more than the sum of their traumas.

Note

1. If you are thoroughly familiar with any of these theories, feel free to skip these summaries or use them as a refresher; they are designed primarily to broaden the perspective of persons not trained in these models.

4

THE MORE TRAUMA-AWARE THEORIES

Although some of the theories presented in Chapter 3 are trauma-aware, in general they do not place trauma as a central theme in their understanding of persons and their struggles. This chapter reviews theories that place relational attachment struggles and traumatic experiences more at the forefront.

Attachment Theory in Greater Detail

Primates—that's us—require secure bonding experiences in infancy to achieve emotion identification and regulation skills, proper brain development, and eventual ability to function reasonably well in relationships with others and socially (Harlow, 2008; Pearlman & Courtois, 2005; A. N. Schore, 2002a, 2002b, 2003a, 2010).

Years of research on infant/caregiver interactions have shown that there are four major ways infants internally organize their sense of attachment (M. D. Ainsworth, 1972; M. D. Ainsworth, Bell, & Stayton, 1972; M. D. S. Ainsworth, Bell, & Stayton, 1974; M. D. S. Ainsworth, Blehar, Waters, & Wall, 1978; M. D. S. Ainsworth & Eichberg, 1991; M. S. Ainsworth, 1979; Bazhenova, Stroganova, Doussard-Roosevelt, Posikera, & Porges, 2007; J. Bowlby, 1978, 1980, 1986, 1988; R. Bowlby, 2004; Duschinsky, 2015; Fosha, 2010; Hesse, 1999):

1. *Securely attached* infants have an internal sense that the caregiver will be available and soothing when they are in distress. Given that

their parental environments provide dependable soothing when the infant/toddler is frightened, these children are not flooded or overwhelmed with anxiety. The caregiver is likely sensitive to how much separation and exploration is safe for this child at this time, and what are the experiences that are "too much" and for which the child must be held, calmed, made safe. Securely attached infants/toddlers come out with the sense that Erikson called "basic trust," the idea that the world can be safe and I can be safe in it. They develop what Bowlby called "a secure base." This felt sense of calm allows exploration, mastery, risk-taking, and the development of an inner confidence that the child can carry as fuel for life. It gives the child a head start on personal strength and social competence and a sense of mastery (M. D. Ainsworth, 1969; M. D. S. Ainsworth et al., 1974; J. Bowlby, 1980; Main, 1995, 2000; Pearlman & Courtois, 2005).

2. *Insecure/dismissive* infants/toddlers have learned that they cannot depend on the caregiver for dependable security. The caregiver may be cold, rejecting, or simply unskilled in knowing what would make the child feel better. The caregiver may be insecurely attached him or herself. They may vacillate. They may appear incompetent even to the infant/toddler. They are in any case undependable, can't be counted on; they allow the child to be flooded by fear and anxiety. In this kind of caregiving environment, some children, whether temperamentally or through other available models, grow dismissive. The internal attitude becomes "no one is to be depended on." "I am better off only depending on myself." "I had better turn around and take care of Mom or Dad so maybe he/she can then care for me." They may become parentified, or sarcastically dismissive of the possibility of a safe primary relationship. They may become guarded, suspicious, isolated, superior, condemning. They are hard to get close to, dismissive of the need for warmth, and often scornful.

3. *Insecure-Ambivalent* infants/toddlers have also been subjected to undependable caretaking, but this caretaking may have been different from that received by the dismissive child. Perhaps the caregiver was sometimes safe and other times rejecting and scornful. Perhaps

sometimes competent and other times overwhelmed. Perhaps not close enough one minute and overwhelming the child with too much protection the next. Here, the child learns to both hope for and expect disappointment in their attempts at attachment. They reach out ambivalently. They are open to attachment one minute and afraid to accept it the next. They are one minute sure of deep acceptance and the next convinced of deep rejection. They want relationships but fight and distrust them. They are often preoccupied with whether those around them are truly attached to them, and pose tests for said persons. This style has sometimes been called *insecure/preoccupied* to reflect the client's constant over-concern over the state of attachments.

4. *Disorganized attachment* children live in a world where there is no predictability. No behavior works to produce safe attachment. No behavioral strategy produces dependable warmth. These children may try everything—be all over the map—and never find anything that works. The world remains terrifying, flooding the child with anxiety, making it impossible to find someplace to settle, creating disorganized, overwhelmed, unpredictable children whose behavior, language, and interpersonal reactions are seemingly incoherent. In such an environment, children with appropriate genetic capacities can become dissociative—in effect creating islets of different response types as situations seem to demand. Do this enough times, through enough terrifying situations, and one can create an islet with a history and a sense of self—an alternative self who deals with frightening Mommy, another one who cares for collapsed Mommy, one who runs and hides from angry Daddy, and so on. Not all disorganized infants and toddlers come out dissociative. This requires certain genetic abilities. But all dissociative clients appear to have come from a disorganized attachment background.

No category system completely accounts for every possible available variation of human behavior without large portions of potential explanation being left out. So, it is possible for people to have a major attachment categorization, with portions of the minor ones also.

One can be insecure/dismissive with a dose of disorganization. Or disorganized with a high dose of dismissive, etc.

The clinical usefulness of the attachment framework is in helping therapists to identify the client's primary relationship metaphor (or Inner Working Model [IWM] per Bowlby), which they are certain to bring into the treatment room. This working model diagnosis can then help in consciously planning the relational stance to be taken with this client. We are likely to behave very differently when the core problem is ambivalence about attachment, from how we would if the person is primarily dismissive. More discussion about this topic occurs later when we talk treatment.

Psychological Trauma and Current Neuroscience

In the introduction, some of the complexities of defining trauma were discussed, and also some human feelings that are *not* trauma. Trauma is not disappointment. It is not being treated insensitively. It is not being exposed to thoughts or beliefs that challenge one's unexamined thinking patterns. One of the best definitions I have heard is that trauma *is exposure to overwhelming and uncontrollable events and feelings for which one is not effectively soothed.*

There is a common successful pattern in parental responses to a child's fear or terror. The toddler is picked up. There is soothing eye contact (Stephen W. Porges, 2003a; S. W. Porges, 2005; Stephen W. Porges, 2011). Maybe the parent rubs the child's back, sings them a song, bounces them, makes soothing sounds, shushes them. Matches their breathing and then slows it down by mutual regulation. The child is made safe and calm. The child learns that life and people can be dependable. Calming neurotransmitters flow around the bloodstream and to the nervous system. The child gets a basic sense of "I'm going to be OK and the world is going to be safe for me to be in."

When parental soothing is ineffective, both the child's nervous system and their developing core conceptualizations about the world (IWMs) are affected. The nervous system stays on overdrive, with epigenetic and priming effects. The child's brain becomes sensitized to and over-alert for symptoms of danger, and their filter system becomes hypervigilant for likely trouble. A student once expressed this by saying a child's walk through a beautiful field of daisies is very different if that child is allergic to bees.

Here's an example of what poor soothing can look like:

> I and my family and children were visiting a butterfly park, where hundreds of beautiful butterflies flew freely in a terrarium-like, multi-acre setting. Near us was a little girl, perhaps 2 years old, screaming in terror as the insects darted about, sometimes landing on her. Her face wore the mask of horror. She screamed and screamed, continually escalating her pitch, and her entire body demanding to be protected. Arms up, face turned towards her mother, terror-stricken. This child's ability not to feel flooded, and like she was breaking into pieces, to calm herself, was shattered. In this case, the mother did nothing, chatted with another mother, drank her coffee, and ignored the child, whose behavior continued to escalate. For that child, this visit to Butterfly Magic was traumatic. Had the primary attachment object, here clearly the mother, responded by the natural act of picking the child up, rubbing her back, making soothing vocal tones or song phrases, helping the child's breathing re-regulate, making eye contact with the child while trying to calm, the experience would not have been a trauma.

So, in the most distilled sense, trauma has two components, an overwhelming and uncontrollable experience, and a failure of soothing. Modern neuroscience has given us some insights about what happens when a stimulus that overwhelms the nervous system is not calmed.

For a fuller exploration, two recent books on the subject, Bessel van der Kolk's "The Body Keeps the Score," and Frewen and Lanius's "Healing the Traumatized Self" (Frewen & Lanius, 2015; van der Kolk, 2014) provide accessible descriptions.

The basic neurobiological outline is as follows:

As briefly discussed in the introduction, the brain can roughly be divided into three major sections:

1. *The brain stem*, existing at the top of the spinal cord, and responsible primarily for automatic processes such as chemical balance, hunger, arousal, sleeping, waking, and breathing (van der Kolk, 2014, p. 59).
2. *The limbic system*, home of fear perception, emotional relevance, perception, and categorization. The amygdala, hippocampus, thalamus, hypothalamus, and sometimes, parts of the prefrontal cortex are considered to make up the limbic system.
3. *The cortex*, home of executive functioning, including inhibiting unwise actions, empathy, planning, time, the context of actions, and making meanings.

Van der Kolk explains what happens in the psychological trauma response: "Whenever the limbic system decides that something is a question of life or death, the pathways between the frontal lobes and the limbic system become extremely tenuous" (p. 64). Two major reactions occur: The person either becomes:

1. overwhelmed by feelings he or she is incapable of managing with conscious thought—the re-experiencing symptoms, hypervigilance, flashbacks, loss of present time (hyperarousal)—or;
2. emotional processes and awareness are dramatically reduced and they become numb and disconnected—the dissociative, depersonalization, and de-realization symptoms (hypo-arousal) (R. Lanius et al., 2010).

Very often, vacillation or alternation occurs between the *hyper-aroused* or *hypo-aroused* responses. Thus, within the posttraumatic stress disorder (PTSD) diagnosis, there exist periods of over-arousal as well as periods of psychological numbing. It seems that different people trend more towards one dominant type of reaction, but in my experience and in the PTSD criteria, we see both—terror where none is needed, freezing where there may be no threat.

The Dissociative Subtype of PTSD: Lanius's and Frewen's Work

So, we have seen that two main physiological reactions to psychological trauma have been identified. In some cases, traumatized people become hypervigilant and over-reactive. In other cases, they become hypo- (under) reactive, and brain centers involved with awareness and conscious thought down-regulate—they dissociate.

Great controversy in the field exists about whether traumatized persons become hypervigilant, with far better recall for traumatic events, or whether they react with inaccessible memories and dissociation from the traumatic events. The conflict has sometimes been referred to as the "repressed memory wars." An entire society, the False Memory Society, was created whose position was that non-continuous memories of trauma were false and implanted by naïve therapists. The controversy generated books, seminars, legal cases, and media reports. A search of the PsychInfo database finds 1,158 references to this controversy. It has been a very big deal. A very limited subset of references follows: (Brenneis, 1997; Ceci, Huffman, Smith, & Loftus, 1994, 1996; Ceci & Loftus, 1994) (Ceci & Bruck, 1995; C. A. Courtois, 1997a, 1999, 2001; C. J. Dalenberg, 1994; Dammeyer, Nightingale, & McCoy, 1997; J. L. Herman & Schatzow, 1987; Loftus, 2003; McNally, 2003; Ornstein, Ceci, & Loftus, 1998a, 1998b; K. S. Pope & Brown, 1996a, 1996b, 1996c; Spanos, 1996a, 1996b, 1996c).

Thus, brain research showing that both hyperarousal and hypoarousal occur in traumatized subjects was groundbreaking. It was this experimental finding that eventually led to the adoption of a dissociative subtype of PTSD in the *DSM-V* (R. Lanius et al., 2010).

Lanius and colleagues used script-driven imagery to trauma survivors in fMRI machines. Essentially, subjects were read a script that described their trauma while the fMRI measured their physiological reactions.

Traumatized persons who became flooded and re-experienced their traumatic events in the fMRI showed a pattern of down-regulation of brain centers (↓rostral anterior cingulate and medial prefrontal cortex) that modulate emotional states—their abilities to "turn down" their fears were compromised. At the same time, one of the major brain regions controlling fear, the amygdala, was up-regulated, along with a region known to control awareness of bodily states (right anterior insula). These individuals became overwhelmed with fear and overly aware of their body's fear signals. In clinical terms, they were provoked into flashbacks and other re-experiencing or remembering phenomena.

On the other hand, persons who dissociated showed opposite brain reactions. The centers that can inhibit emotion and arousal were up-regulated. They, in turn, modulated/turned down the emotions too much, and this resulted in decreased fear and decreased bodily awareness. And so, their brains effectively turned off and numbed out their reactions to the trauma.

Research showed that approximately 70% of Lanius and colleagues' subjects reacted in the hypervigilant manner, whereas about 30% reacted in the dissociative pattern (Frewen, 2015). So here we have a potential resolution of the "everybody remembers their traumas, there's no such thing as dissociation" vs. "people dissociate their traumas" controversy. Subjects in their experiments appeared to do both. It is not clear right now whether persons characteristically become either the hyper- or hypo-aroused type of responder, as a result of situational, developmental or other factors, or whether they vacillate. The classic symptom configuration of PTSD would hold that persons do some of each, with conceptions of trauma now resting on a four-pronged model. Per the *DSM-V* definition of PTSD, persons with PTSD have symptoms in the following four categories:

1. Intrusive, distressing memories (flashbacks)
2. Avoidance of trauma-linked reminders
3. Negative effects on their cognitions, mood, and sense of self
4. Marked changes in arousal

The dissociative subtype of PTSD includes these, plus symptoms of depersonalization (the events feel distant from the self) or derealization (the events do not seem real) (American Psychiatric Association, 2013).

Advances in neuroscience in the past several decades have helped us understand more of the development of emotion regulation in children, the workings of emotion regulation in adults, and how people influence each other's emotional states, sometimes called *mutual regulation*. Some of these advances are described in the next section.

Neuroscience and Interpersonal Neurobiology

Human interactions affect us on a biological and neurochemical level. The field of interpersonal neurobiology has emerged to study these interactions. As we interact with others, they have an influence on the neurotransmitters we produce, and vice versa. In a conversation, we mutually co-regulate each other. Similarly to the parent-infant interaction, we may calm another when they are upset, do nothing, or frighten/hurt them further. Our personal emotion regulation systems change because of these interactions, particularly if there are patterns of repeated interactions. Biological structures in the brain change depending on our interpersonal experiences (Mickleborough et al., 2011; A. N. Schore & McIntosh, 2011; A. N. Schore, 1991, 1994, 1996, 2000a, 2000b, 2001a, 2001b, 2002b, 2003a, 2003b, 2009a, 2009b; Siegel, 1999, 2001, 2002, 2004, 2012a, 2012b).

In a seminal work, Allan Schore has described "the science of the art of psychotherapy" (A. Schore, 2012). The crucial point for therapist development is that the nature of the relationship we provide has physiological/neurobiological effects. The therapy relationship changes the brain of the traumatized patient if we are properly tuned in, responsive, and soothing—a safe container for their experiences. Much of this is nonverbal, happening between the right-brain of the therapist and the client. How we *are* is communicated to the client in an implicit fashion. The client similarly influences the therapist's right brain. A major job of the therapist is to strive to become mindful of how the patient is affecting our affective state, and how we are affecting theirs.

Interpersonal neurobiology is a vast and ever-growing field, and this is not a comprehensive review by any means. The point for the current work is our need as therapists to provide an environment that aids and produces decreases in fear, terror, and freezing in our traumatized clients.

Good evidence exists that provision of effective therapy changes brains (Chalavi et al., 2015; A. N. Schore, 2000a, 2010, 2011; J. R. Schore & Schore, 2008; van der Hart, Nijenhuis, & Solomon, 2010).

Polyvagel theory, discussed next, is another neuroscience perspective helpful to therapists in case conceptualization; it is an additional useful lens.

Current Neuroscience: Polyvagal Theory

Porges has contributed to much of the work just discussed by helping us to understand how the human infant develops a system of social engagement with others (S. W. Porges, 2003b, 2005, 2009, 2011). The material that is of essential use to trauma therapists is the description of how eye contact, tone of voice, facial expression, and the rhythm and melody of speech are read by the child's brain as indications of safety or threat. And the "reading devices" in the brain are connected physiologically to the heart and other internal organs. So there are physiological reactions beyond just fight/flight when the child is scared. *There is a closing off of ability to connect with others until there is effective soothing.* For the therapist, we are not often conscious of how powerfully the rhythms of our speech, the rate of our breathing, and the tone of our voice are our therapeutic tools. Likely, most of us have made unconscious adjustments to our daily speech rhythm and tone of voice to match what the client seems to need. A close reading of Dr. Porges's work suggests that therapists need to pay more conscious attention to the use of these physiological mutual regulators in their work in general, but especially with a traumatized client. It suggests that if we can aid a client to calm, by use of such tools, then we move the client towards being accessible to relational repair. *How we are with them sends a message of how the current world is/can be safer than the world they grew up in.* And it starts in the therapeutic office and then can generalize into their entire worldview. We begin the journey from insecure or chaotic attachment to secure attachment by how we are, and who we are, and what we are like, with our clients.

Often for unknown reasons, useful perspectives seem to "go out of style" and are referenced and taught less often than in the past. Our next topic, hypnotizability and dissociative ability, was at one time at the forefront of complex trauma treatment (R. P. Kluft, 1985, 2012a, 2012b, 2015; Landry & Raz, 2015; Levin et al., 2013; Lichtenberg et al., 2008; Lifshitz,

Campbell, & Raz, 2012; Raz, 2007, 2011, 2012). It is still taught now, but appears less central. The next section briefly reviews the contributions of these topics to our diagnostic thinking and therapeutic practice.

Hypnotizability and Dissociative Ability

One of the major mysteries in reactions to chronic traumatization is the question of what occurs when behavior takes place outside of the individual's conscious awareness. Why do some people lose current time perspective and react as if the traumas were occurring in real time (i.e., flashbacks)? Why do some lose any sense of personal volition in their trauma reactions (dissociate)? Why do dissociative persons believe they have amnesia for certain events, when lab studies of information transfer show that events are learned across alleged dissociative barriers (Dorahy et al., 2014)?

Some of the variability in how trauma survivors react (especially those with a complex or dissociative adaptation) is due to their inherent abilities to self-hypnotize and/or dissociate in response to traumatic events or reminders of them. Good evidence exists for inherent genetic variability in hypnotizability (Raz, 2005, 2007, 2012). The higher the genetic ability to use self-hypnosis in coping with traumatic events, the more likely it will be that a person can use dissociative defenses as a refuge and escape from the trauma (R. P. Kluft, Kinsler, O'Neil, J., 2014).

Neuroimaging studies of the behavior of subjects under hypnosis who "involuntarily" move their limbs in response to hypnotic suggestion provide clues to this phenomenon. There appears to be a decoupling of control and monitoring processes. Areas of the prefrontal cortex involved with selection and implementation of responses are decoupled from areas of the anterior cingulate cortex that are involved in the person's sense of agency or self-control. "Specifically, without proper monitoring feedback, the implementation of hypnotic responses is less attributable to the self and remains beyond subjective feelings of control" (Landry & Raz, 2015, p. 304).

As briefly discussed previously, a substantial number of persons who have experienced trauma dissociate—they have reduced awareness of their actions and feelings. Some lose the sense of time. Some lose the sense of control of their actions. Some develop repeated patterns of dealing with trauma that can lead to a sense of a different self with a different history and different characteristics. In some cases, persons develop numbers of alternate senses of self in what is termed *dissociative identity disorder* (DID). Others experience primarily the sense of being distant from their own experiences, which do not feel real. This is the experience of *derealization*. Others feel as if the experiences are not happening to them. This is the phenomenon of *depersonalization*. The abilities to use these dissociative defenses depend in large part on the client's self-hypnosis capacity.

Paradoxically and importantly, the innate capacities for self-hypnosis, and for dissociation, can be used for healing. In addition to the symptom-generating aspects of loss of sense of agency (depersonalization, derealization, dissociative alter states), hypnosis can play an important part in teaching calming, in working through traumatic events at "volumes" that the nervous system can digest, in managing flashbacks, in ego-strengthening, and in teaching a sense of control to patients when they feel out of control. We return to this in more detail as we discuss specific phases of treatment.

Betrayal Trauma

Human infants are hard-wired for connection. Infants are born mostly incapable of anything beyond crying and suckling and sleeping. Babies are also extremely talented at peeing and pooping, and hopefully developing. That development depends first, on physical safety. Then on being fed, and protected from the elements, disease, and predators, among other things. If we are to develop properly, we also need protection from inconsolable terror/anxiety, which affects brain development (R. Bowlby, 2004; Harlow, 1997; Harlow & Zimmermann, 1996; S. W. Porges & Furman, 2011). The main roles of the primary caretaker, most often the mother, are to provide the safety and proper environment for development that the infant needs.

What happens if the major sources of safety are also the sources of threat and trauma? A sometimes-soothing mother also rejects and acts cold to the child, or beats them, neglects to feed them, leaves them in a dirty diaper in the crib for hours? A father cuddles but also sexually abuses? A grandparent buys toys and ice cream but also both sexually abuses the child and lets others do so?

How the child reacts depends in part on the innate capacities of the child. Some may have an easy temperament and respond resiliently, and perhaps be "delightful" enough that the child can spontaneously decrease the threat from outside. This is not to say that a child is responsible for fixing a hostile external environment. It is merely to acknowledge that certain infants have inborn biology that gifts them with the abilities to pull the best possible from the environment.

However, for most children, it is a terrifying trap to be dependent on ones who are physically and emotionally harmful. It is the essence of a double bind. The child needs the parent, but the parent also hurts them. How does a child cope in such a circumstance?

Several theorists have made it clear that children often resort to self-blame in their attempts to understand this double-bind and make the world less terrifying (J. J. Freyd, 1996; J. J. Freyd, & Birrell, 2013; Janoff-Bulman & McPherson Frantz, 1997; Nathanson, 1997a). This maintains the illusion that the world *can be safe—if only the child were __. (Fill in the blank with any qualities the child may feel would please the adult better.)* Self-blame preserves the illusion that the child has control of their environment. If only he or she was more athletic, prettier, smarter, better behaved, took care of Daddy or Mommy better, home with them could be safe. This is a mental escape from the inescapable double bind of being betrayed by loved ones on whom the child is dependent (J. J. Freyd, 1996; J. J. Freyd & Birrell, 2013).

Another coping method that has been identified involves forgetting, specifically not remembering the terrifying or otherwise harmful behaviors of the betraying attachment figure. It seems that the ability to not-remember is made easier for persons with innate capacities for self-hypnosis and dissociative reactions (Frewen, 2015; R. A. Lanius et al., 2014).

Freyd and colleagues have shown that, although all traumatic events do not necessarily lead either to psychopathology or memory difficulties, traumas that involve betrayal by a figure who is necessary for the safety and biological development of the child are especially difficult and harm-inducing (J. J. Freyd, 1996; J. J. Freyd & Birrell, 2013). *And it is this paradox that relational therapy for complex trauma deals with.*

The therapeutic relationship becomes a learning laboratory for a non-betraying primary relationship. Although it is never possible to give a client a new set of parents, or a new past, one can begin to change the lenses through which the person looks at the world. Hopefully the therapy can help move the client from viewing the world as betraying and eternally dangerous, to viewing the world as a "possibly, sometimes, with certain people, maybe if I let them in a bit" safer world. And as this happens, the client becomes easier to relate to by outside parties, their world expands, better relationships can hopefully form, and the door is opened out of the paradox of self-hate towards "maybe I'm good enough, maybe the world is safe enough." And this is the task of relational trauma therapy. Let's look more deeply into the core experience of shame and self-loathing as the "solution" to betrayal trauma.

The Core Experience of Shame and Self-Loathing

As briefly mentioned in the introduction, human beings try to make sense of horrid experiences (Frankl, 1997; Janoff-Bulman, 1992; Janoff-Bulman & Thomas, 1989; Janoff-Bulman & Timko, 1987). As previously stated, one of the best ways to do this is to *blame yourself.* How does this make sense? Quite a number of things can go wrong if one blames the perpetrator. If I am small and/or vulnerable and blame the perpetrator, he or she could hurt me more physically or emotionally. He or she could fail to feed, clothe, or shelter me. He or she may withdraw any positive, loving experiences I may have received. He or she may abandon me. He or she may make an alliance with others, perhaps a sibling or another adult, to view me unfavorably and to scapegoat me or further victimize me. And, of course, I may come to feel completely out of control of my world, with a shattering of any conviction that the world makes sense. I may become flooded with panic and debilitating anxiety.

Primates are biologically determined to want and need parental attachment. Withdrawal or inconsistency of attachment equals danger and undermines neural development (Harlow, 1997; Meyer, Novak, Bowman, & Harlow, 1975; A. N. Schore, 2000a, 2001a, 2002a; J. R. Schore & Schore, 2008; Suomi & Harlow, 1977; van der Kolk, 2004).

To avoid these dangers, what can a child do? *Shame and self-blame are exceedingly helpful in preserving the illusion that the world can be a safe place* (Janoff-Bulman, 1992). If I blame myself, I can maintain the illusion that the world could be safe. I maintain some control. The thought pattern can become "If only I was better, this would not happen." If I become ashamed of *myself* there is possibly something I could *do* about what is happening to me. "If only I were a better _____, Daddy or Mommy or Uncle Ron would love me and not treat me this way." Being "better" is something I can strive for, work towards, have power over. I can obtain a helpful illusion that there is safety "out there" if only *I* were somehow different. Placing the blame on me paradoxically makes the world a "safer" place. *Intense shame is a solution to childhood terror.*

Shame also has the characteristic of turning off other emotions and behaviors. It is the equivalent of the puppy offering up its belly or neck to the alpha dog. It both turns off whatever behavior might have provoked the attack, and offers vulnerability to signal the perpetrator that further attacks are unnecessary to obtain my submission. *Shame makes me safer* (Nathanson, 1987, 1997a, 1997b).

One of the central tasks of therapy with complex trauma survivors is reducing the sense of shame and increasing the sense of worth, of personal value, of being a "good enough" person (P. J. Kinsler, 1992; P. J. Kinsler et al., 2009; Winnicott, 1957a, 1957b, 1958, 1965). Pride in oneself contradicts and hopefully extinguishes the sense of badness and self-hatred that are so common in abuse survivors.

A first principle of relationship-based trauma therapy is to work towards reducing shame. Any response the therapist (or anyone else of significance for that matter) makes that helps the client feel less loathsome is effective therapy.

Let's look at one way of using all these diagnostic lenses discussed previously, all the layers of the onion, in a working diagnostic conceptualization of a client:

Case Example: A Multi-Lens Diagnostic Conceptualization of a Client

I knew this client before I knew this client. That is, she was the patient of another therapist in our shared office suite. I'd pass her in the waiting room—and frankly from what I observed—was happy she wasn't mine. Oh, I know we're not supposed to say things like that—but they happen. Whether we have prior knowledge of the person, or none, we do quick "sizing-up." It's part of our "is this a saber tooth tiger or just a puppy" threat evaluation system.

This person looked *angry*. Agitated, nervous, explosive, hard to please, dangerous. All assessments I made from observations of pursed lips, chair squirming, tensed shoulders, hands nervously tapping armrests, and sometimes rolling eyes.

So, of course, life being life, her therapist left the practice and moved—and I was the other trauma therapist in town. Having been close to that therapist, and knowing that she had accepted difficult referrals when I was full, I agreed to take the patient on. So, my first diagnostic task was to *make overt to myself the hunches and prejudices I was already working under.* And this is a first task in all diagnoses, because we come to the diagnostic process with both conscious and implicit biases, whether of social class—a taboo to talk about in our society—ethnicity, race, religion, behavior. We make quick assumptions based on how the referral came in, what the person sounded like on the answering machine, what our secretary or scheduler clued us in to, and what our initial physical and psychological impressions were. And we bring along the baggage of our own personal history dependent, and likely weirdly carved lenses from our past.

And so, the first task is *noting what's going on with us and setting aside all the foregoing.* They need to go in to an internal folder labeled "crazy hypotheses I have formed or malformed with terribly inadequate information." And we all better have or develop that folder. But also, we had best not forget these first impressions—because they are also likely to be what others see, hear, and respond to, and may be how the client "provokes" reactions in others, either on an occasional or more frequent basis. For me it is a mental discipline to actively bring these implicit assumptions to my awareness, and then to deliberately push them off to the side or to the back of my mind to reflect on later.

So, the first diagnostic task is in the therapist. And with the patient in question, I worked to put the baggage away, and to take in and come to know the person in more open ways. And so, I looked at the layers . . .

From a biological potential, likely genetic perspective, just as part of the intake information gathering, I soon learned that Laurie (a pseudo name used with permission) had a master's degree. So, some clear intellectual ability and some shared assumptions about the value of education. I learned her father was a college administrator in a high position. From this I could infer some familial pressure to excel educationally—and ask myself whether a master's might not have been enough in her family. I learned that she had a responsible position in a social service agency—when she wasn't in the hospital for chronic suicide attempts. How to make sense of this major discrepancy? How could I, and we, understand it? At the very least, grit, persistence, achievement orientation, and not giving up in the face of severe psychiatric problems were all in the mix. And I learned she was the primary support of a family with several children and a husband who was chronically under-employed, and seemed to be verbally aggressive at home to her and the children. From that bit of information, I made a hypothesis based on family systems theory, that both her function and dysfunction might be important to the configuration of the power structure within the family—and that the struggle over this power structure was likely to be a trial for her children.

Going deeper, here was a person with an intact family but a history of chronic depression. She was a person who self-mutilated by cutting herself repeatedly with knives. She made dramatic and dangerous suicide attempts, including driving her car into a tree and having to be extracted by the "jaws of life." Chronically cutting herself and making serious suicide attempts, depression, a prior history of failed treatment, and a tenuous primary relationship all suggested complex trauma in her history.

Marriage to a highly critical husband led me to add the intrapsychic to the systems analysis. What were this woman's developmental lessons about self-assertion and autonomy? What were her lessons about feeling and expressing anger? What about her abilities to advocate for her own needs? How low was her self-esteem regarding her relational worth to a spouse/partner? How did this fit together with her apparent occupational self-regard, which had allowed her to "go places"? What were the internal conflicts that led to repetitive unraveling and suicidality? Were there traumatic experiences that led to a mismatch between educational and social/familial success? What were the larger family systems pressures that seemed to be keeping her in role and were likely contributing to her depression?

What was the family of origin mental health history like? Was everyone chronically depressed? From the learning by imitation perspective, how did her mother model being a woman? How did her father model being a male? What were the sources of her pain and satisfaction as she grew up in that family? Did anyone soothe her? Did she have to compartmentalize memories or relationships to survive in that family? Was there betrayal and by whom?

Were there larger social system issues that could help or hurt the therapy? For example, as I found out later, the family had a huge New England Yankee tradition. Self-reliance, frugality, stoicism, persistence despite obstacles, tolerance of pain—these were in the DNA of this family from Plymouth Rock to my therapy room. It was crucial to know about them, because they were bedrock, and this client could not collapse below this granite shelf. It was always there to draw upon and was in fact fuel for getting by and eventually getting through.

I was to learn that Laurie did, in fact have a history of chronic intrafamilial abuse. Tragically, she had a long history of sexual and emotional abuse by a father who was a "pillar of the community," and a mother who "half-knew but made sure not to know" to preserve the family and its social and financial status. This type of paternal incest is among the most complex and complicated traumas that can befall a child and leads them to use extreme defensive operations to cope (Courtois, 2010; Terr, 1990). For example, this ongoing parental betrayal set the stage for dissociation, for eventual development into a less than wholly integrated person. I eventually found that Laurie had educated and achievement-oriented parts of her mind—dissociated alter selves—and they allowed her to function well in her occupational life. She also had abused, devalued, "unworthy" but desperately hurt and angry parts who, it turned out, were what I had attuned and reacted to when I saw her in the waiting room. And when these parts pushed their pain to the surface, she had tremendous anxiety, terror of betraying family secrets, hatred towards herself for breaking the family rules when she disclosed the abuse in therapy, and profound grief. These were, in part, what led to the suicidal times.

Seeing these aspects of Laurie was something like a three-dimensional (or n-dimensional) chess game, with everything from biological endowment to familial social history representing the dimensions. And her therapy required work on all these dimensions eventually; we return to this case history later in the book.

5

WHAT CAN WE LEARN
FROM OUTCOME STUDIES
OF PSYCHOTHERAPY?

The study of the effectiveness of psychotherapy (referred to as *psychotherapy outcome research*) began during World War I (Pfister, 1917). Although there were numerous prior individual studies, by the 1970s, a statistical method called *meta-analysis* had been developed to allow the combining of individual studies into a general statistically accurate summary of the effects of therapy (M. L. Smith & Glass, 1977).

In the Smith and Glass seminal paper referenced above, they found that good old individual person-to-person therapy works. Carl Rogers' initial development of the facilitative conditions for effective therapy was not armchair theorizing. The conditions were derived from research studies asking patients with successful therapies to try to drill down to the factors that made therapy successful (Raskin & Rogers, 2005; Rogers, 1975, 2007a, 2007b). These studies included audio-taping the sessions of therapists in training and rating the tapes to determine if the novice therapists provided the facilitative conditions and/or could be trained to do so (Carkhuff, 1969; Carkhuff, Kratochvil, & Friel, 1968; Carkhuff & Truax, 1965, 1966; Truax & Carkhuff, 1967). As a graduate student, I was lucky enough to have this experience, which ultimately led me to be so interested in the relational aspects of therapy. The experience of first receiving relational therapy (P. Kinsler, 2016) and then learning how to perform it led to an abiding interest in conflicts within the field between behavioral and relational models. These are discussed further in this chapter.

The Behavioral Versus Relational War and Its Resolution

During the entire time I have been in practice, there has been an ongoing war between behavioral and relational thinkers, both in attempting to explain human behavior and in developing models of healing and therapy drawn from these explanatory systems. The competition goes on today between the exposure-model therapies for trauma and the relationship-based ones. The history of this conflict is covered in a wonderful paper by Adam Horvath called "You Can't Step Into the Same River Twice, but You Can Stub Your Toes on the Same Rock: Psychotherapy Outcome From a 50-Year Perspective" (Horvath, 2013). Horvath traces a hotly contested debate between two eminent psychologists Hans Eysenck (Eysenck, 1952) and Hans Strupp (Strupp, 1963, 1964, 1973a), who held two very different perspectives. Eysenck long argued that thinking of client problems in terms of their mental processes did not yield therapy that worked and advocated for the development of purely behavioral therapies that he viewed as essential and as the only scientific approach. "They promised to build the edifice of the science of behavior by expunging all references to 'mentalistic concepts' that, they argued, formed the shaky foundations of psychoanalytic psychology" (Horvath, 2013, p. 26). Strupp essentially believed that a person's inner world and mental processes determined behavior and were changeable by therapy (Strupp, 1962, 1963, 1967, 1970, 1971, 1972, 1973b).

However, after the publication of the Smith and Glass meta-analytic paper on the effects of psychotherapy and the components that contribute to effectiveness (1977), the argument over *whether* psychotherapy based on psychodynamic concepts worked changed at least somewhat, to focus on the specific components of psychotherapy that worked. There was "growing acceptance of the idea that *the relationship in therapy between helper and client is a generic element that plays an important role in making all forms of psychotherapy, and indeed . . . all human to human helping endeavors, work*" (Horvath, 2013, p. 28).

This general agreement that psychotherapy works and that the relationship between therapist and client is central led the American Psychological Association to pass a formal resolution that psychotherapy was effective in remediating a variety of mental health and psychosocial concerns. It took the authors of the resolution 27 uses of "Whereas" to reach one "Therefore," as follows:

> Therefore: Be It Resolved that, as a healing practice and professional service, psychotherapy is effective and highly cost-effective. In controlled trials and in clinical practice, psychotherapy results in benefits that markedly exceed those experienced by individuals who need mental health services but do not receive psychotherapy. Consequently, psychotherapy should be included in the health care system as an established evidence-based practice.
>
> (American Psychological Association, 2013, p. 320)

The agreement that psychotherapy works led the APA to appoint task forces to specify what contributed to its effectiveness. Here are the relevant conclusions of the 2011 task force:

- The therapy relationship makes substantial and consistent contributions to psychotherapy outcome independent of the specific types of treatment.
- The therapy relationship accounts for why clients improve (or fail to improve) at least as much as the particular treatment method.
- Practice and treatment guidelines should explicitly address therapist behaviors and qualities that promote a facilitative therapy relationship.
- Efforts to promulgate best practices or evidence-based practices (EBPs) without including the relationship are seriously incomplete and potentially misleading.
- Adapting or tailoring the therapy relationship to specific patient characteristics (in addition to diagnosis) enhances the effectiveness of treatment.

- The therapy relationship acts in concert with treatment methods, patient characteristics, and practitioner qualities in determining effectiveness; a comprehensive understanding of effective (and ineffective) psychotherapy will consider all of these determinants and their optimum combinations (Norcross & Wampold, 2011, p. 98).

For working trauma therapists, this might be a good list to send to managed-care companies when use of relationship-based therapy is challenged.

What Kind of Relationships Do and Don't Work?

The APA resolution just cited goes on to say that the following factors are "demonstrably effective" elements of the therapy relationship:

- Alliance in individual psychotherapy
- Alliance in youth psychotherapy
- Alliance in family therapy
- Cohesion in group therapy
- Empathy
- Collecting client feedback

(Norcross & Wampold, 2011, p. 99)

These relational elements are important to the success of all psychotherapy, and I consider them especially important for trauma therapies.

Early in my struggles to conceptualize what appeared to be working when providing complex trauma therapy, it became clear that the relationship was especially predictive. Good and safe and bounded relationships worked. Chaotic, confused, negative, or only technical relationships did not. I published a paper entitled "The Centrality of Relationship: What's not being said" in 1992 (P. J. Kinsler, 1992). That paper became the focus of an issue of the journal *Dissociation*, and was responded to with perhaps more heat than light. Arguments developed whether the specific therapeutic techniques were most important in producing change for complex trauma clients, or whether the relationship variable was of core importance. I have noted a movement, over more than 20 years, towards acknowledgment of the importance, the centrality, of the relational variable. This is not to say that technique is unimportant. Therapists must know both *what to do (techniques) and what kind of relationships to do it in.*

In addition to the general research just discussed demonstrating how important relational variables are to general psychotherapy outcome, relational variables have also been found to be of great importance in working with complex trauma survivors.

For example, Dalenberg has found that therapist openness, especially about when they are frustrated by clients, strongly influences clients' ratings of the effectiveness of their therapies. Bethany Brand and colleagues have studied outcome of therapy for dissociative disorders and found that client ratings of the therapy relationship are strongly predictive of therapy outcome (Brand et al., 2012; Carlson & Dalenberg, 2000; C. Dalenberg, 2014; C. J. Dalenberg, 2004; Dorahy et al., 2014). Relationship issues are demonstrably important in the success of trauma psychotherapy.

Let's look at the now consensus model of how this is accomplished (C. A. Courtois, 1999), always acknowledging that models are intellectual schemas, not religions or invariable procedures.

6
THE THREE-STAGE CONSENSUS
MODEL OF TREATMENT

Complex psychological trauma can cause symptoms and struggles in all major areas of life, from psychiatric symptoms to general health effects, to effects on all our human relationships, to our attitudes towards ourselves.

In the introductory chapter, four core areas of posttraumatic symptom formation were discussed. To review, these are issues of psychological intrusions such as flashbacks or daytime revivifications of the trauma. There are issues of numbing of responsiveness and awareness. There are startle reactions and constant anxiety, tension, and anticipation of danger (hyperarousal). There are changes in personality formation and how a survivor feels about him or herself. There is the burden of intense shame and self-hate.

A chronically suicidal worldview can develop—no one and nothing is safe and ending life is the only way to stop the pain. Self-mutilation may occur. Often there are repeated psychiatric hospitalizations.

Complex trauma survivors may be plagued by the sense of being damaged goods, and of always having their trauma-based symptoms interfere with their efforts to establish occupational or relational safety and stability. The effects are profound and encompass vast portions of the entire terrain of life.

A number of writers and professional societies have developed a consensus model for the treatment of complex trauma and/or dissociation.

This chapter provides a brief guide to this overall model, upon which the later presentation of the six relational crises rests.

It is central to remember that treatments that flow like a river gently to the sea are the exception rather than the rule. All treatment models need to be adapted to the actual human client in front of us.

Kluft has identified three major trajectories in treatment of complex trauma, essentially:

1. Rapid, hard-working, and with relatively quick change
2. Slow-moving over the course of years, with gradually appreciating change
3. A primarily static and supportive pattern, with perhaps little change (R. P. Kluft, 1994)

Regardless of trajectory, the major societies and theorists writing about trauma treatment have adopted a three-stage model as the relevant conceptual paradigm (Chu, 2011; M. Cloitre et al., 2012; C. A. Courtois, 1997b, 1999; Foa, 2009).

The three stages commonly accepted are:

1. Safety and stabilization
2. Working through and reassessing traumatic memories
3. Community reintegration and connection

Safety and Stabilization

Complex trauma clients often enter therapy with numbers of potentially dangerous and disabling symptoms. Life crises are common. Suicidality is common. Depression, from chronic moderate depression to intense crippling depression, is regularly present. These clients present deficits in self-soothing and tolerance of interpersonal stresses. Sometimes their revivification symptoms can frighten others. Often, job performance follows a sine wave, with periods of competent functioning followed by collapse. The clients sometimes-to-often appear chaotic, especially to the therapist just learning to work with this kind of person.

Before the development of the three-stage model, therapies sometimes replicated chaos rather than calming. Therapists had not gathered enough experience to understand that first, the therapy must establish safety and stabilization skills before delving into so-called 'trauma work.' This is not a book directed at presenting this global model, but a work directed towards a clarification and expansion of the model. Readers are referred particularly to two volumes by Courtois and Ford for explications of the basic model (C. Courtois, & Ford, 2009; C. A. Courtois & Ford, 2013). The origin of the model can be found in Judith Herman's seminal work (Herman, 1992). A special adaptation of the model for work with the dissociative disorders can be found in the guidelines for treatment of this disorder published by the International Society for the Study of Trauma and Dissociation (Chu, 2011).

However, a sketch of what a therapist may do in a safety and stabilization phase is called for. Some of the activities might include:

1. Safety planning with the patient
2. Teaching of self-calming skills
3. Practice in visualization of potentially safe environments
4. Teaching a patient how to monitor their internal processes (i.e., mindfulness)
5. Modeling how a person can contain anxiety and fear
6. Providing a safe-enough therapy relationship so that the client begins to notice and feel the difference between how they were treated in their traumatic experiences and how they are treated in therapy
7. Training the client in methods that will later be used to work on their traumatic memories

For other activities involved in this phase, reference the works cited previously. The safety and stabilization phase is often the longest phase of the three. An anonymous poet once wrote, "A long conviction of worthlessness builds strong walls."

I want to caution readers not to take the model as a therapeutic religion. I have seen cases in which clients who clearly needed some trauma processing to alleviate the steam in their pressure cooker were maltreated by clinicians insisting that they "do their skills," and would not allow the person to talk about their traumas.

This is a model that must be flexibly applied, always considering the condition and needs of the client in the room. For this reason, note that this model is recursive. There are times when, much as one would like to first get safety and stabilization accomplished, one cannot, because the valve on the pressure cooker is shooting off steam, and it becomes necessary to attend to the trauma on a "right now" basis. There are times when one returns to a previous stage should the client, for example, destabilize following a new traumatic event, or as the result of a powerful trigger from an older one, or to a major relationship change in the real world, etc. The guidelines cannot be rigidly applied; they are guides, not rules.

It *is* best, however, to keep the stages in mind while the relational tugs of the therapy pull one towards possibly premature trauma discussions. Clients may destabilize, become self-destructive, suicidal, or more depressed if they are moved towards discussing the traumatic events in their lives without establishment of safety and stability. It is a matter of therapeutic discernment and attunement whether a client simply must talk about trauma to stabilize or re-stabilize, or whether this should be put off in the interest of client safety.

Once safety and stabilization are reasonably solidly established—a judgment that should likely be made in discussion with the client—the treatment turns to working on those traumatic experiences that the client finds necessary to get beyond. Recall, we are trying to help the client get to the "OK, it's been processed by my cortex now; I have context, I have found a way to make sense of and cope with it; it's just a memory now" stage.

The next step is working through and reassessing traumatic memories.

Working Through and Reassessing Traumatic Memories

There are three core components to this stage. The first is the client having some of the emotions connected with the memory in a more muted and tolerable way. This usually encompasses both discussing them while in the presence of a soothing other, and experiencing them in a more calm and relaxed state than when the original trauma occurred. So, we are talking about both reduced intensity and the second aspect, enhanced soothing. A third crucial aspect of the working through involves cortical processing—finding a way to make some sense of the event, to comprehend it, to find a system of meaning that brings it to some level of comprehensibility. In some ways, it is the removal of the awe from something awful, a word that is overused, but taken apart means "full of awe, not comprehendible."

This change is so hard to grasp if one has either not gone through it personally or helped others to. The following is something that might help from history:

> I have previously written of how growing up in an apartment building containing many Holocaust survivors was a formative experience (P. Kinsler, 2016). My grandmother Rose came to the United States in 1908 from a little village in Austria-Hungary. She bemoaned the Holocaust and the loss of her relatives, saying, "How could this happen, in the most well-educated country in Europe?" I could never figure it out either, and I agonized too.
>
> Long after Grandma Rose's death, I read two novels by Herman Wouk, *The Hope*, and *The Glory* (Wouk, 1993, 1994). Wouk essentially proposed that perhaps the Holocaust was the only way for enough sympathy to come forward to allow the Jewish people to re-establish a homeland. Although I'm not sure this explanation, what today we might call a re-frame, resolves the question, it does provide an inkling of how a horrible memory or set of memories can be re-evaluated, reassessed, and thought/felt about differently.

A number of methods exist to help accomplish this reassessment, and more detailed descriptions may be found in the previously referenced works. The following are a few common ways of helping to accomplish this task:

1. *Abreaction and Fractionated Abreaction*
   An abreaction is essentially a cathartic re-experiencing of a traumatic emotion in the presence of a helping other. Because of the

intensity of so many traumatic experiences, Kluft developed the concept of a fractionated abreaction. This is essentially a technique for experiencing piecemeal abreactions at levels that can be tolerated by the client. The goal is tolerable re-experiencing. "The fractionated abreaction involves achieving this goal in small increments" (R. P. Kluft, 1993b).

2. *Eye Movement Desensitization and Reprocessing (EMDR)*

EMDR is a technique that combines a cognitive-behavioral paradigm for changes in thoughts, feelings, and statements about the self, with alternating physical stimulation. The cognitive-behavioral paradigm takes a traumatic memory of somewhat tolerable intensity—not the worst ever. It asks the client-therapist combination to obtain a measure of how distressing the memory is, called *subjective units of distress* (SUDS). The therapist-client dyad determines how the person feels about themselves before processing, such as "I must have done something to deserve this." They then develop how the person would like to feel post-processing: "I was a helpless child but am strong now." The dyad develops a metaphor for the movement through time: "As we go forward through this memory, as the train moves forward down the tracks, you will leave behind the sense of being damaged goods and move towards realizing you were only a helpless child then but are strong now." The client is asked to begin to think about the memory as they move through time, leaving the old conceptualization behind and moving towards the new one. Alternating stimulation via either eye movements, hand taps, or eye-tracking a bar with moving lights is used as the person moves through the memory for a limited time of exposure. After several such exposures, the client is intended to reach a lower sense of distress (SUDS) and to increase their desired and healthier self-concept.

This is the briefest of overviews. Readers are referred to the extensive training programs offered by the EMDR institute and/or to the seminal work in the field by Francine Shapiro (Shapiro, 2001).

3. *Systematic Desensitization*

This technique also uses the concept of graded exposure to the traumatic experience. Clients develop a hierarchy of stimuli that moves from distantly connected to the traumatic experience, towards the experience itself. So, consider someone in a frightening auto accident. A distant stimulus might be approaching the car in the driveway to begin the trip, and the eventual traumatic stimulus could be hearing the metal tearing as the accident occurs. Several steps along that path are developed: getting in the car, beginning to drive to the mall, watching the light turn green, etc. The client is taught a deep relaxation technique such as the one described in "The Relaxation Response" (Benson, 2000). While relaxed, they are exposed to each of the stimulus cards in graded sequence, maintaining the relaxed state, and thus at least in theory removing the connection between the stimulus and the fear response (also called *deconditioning*). For foundational articles on these methods, see the seminal works of Wolpe and co-authors (Wolpe, 1959, 1968, 1969; Wolpe & Lazarus, 1966).

4. *Hypnotic Interventions*

The most recent definition of hypnosis is: "A state of consciousness involving focused attention and reduced peripheral awareness characterized by an enhanced capacity for response to suggestion" (Elkins, 2015). There are many ways hypnosis is and can be effectively used in trauma treatment. Methods such as hypnotic distancing can aid in reducing the intensity of the traumatic experience: "Visualize what happened to you through the wrong end of the binoculars," which can aid in making the memory/visualization less intense. Suggestions/metaphors for containment can help curtail intense traumatic flashbacks: "Picture the memory on a CD disk. Visualize ejecting the CD and the screen goes blank." "Picture putting the CD in a locked bank vault" and so on. Some techniques increase a client's sense of control: "That locked bank vault will only open during our next session. The air lock will only let out exactly the right amount of material which you will be able to cope with." Thus, hypnosis and suggestion are used for intensity reduction, sense of control enhancement, and reassessing the overwhelming nature of the event. Suggestion can also be used to enhance the person's sense of mastery: "Visualize yourself as a grown-up today taking your own power and refusing to be treated that way." The topic of hypnosis is large enough to have generated professional societies and journals; the foregoing examples are meant to provide a taste that may lead the reader to pursue further reading and training. Introductory and intermediate workshops are often offered at the conferences of the International Society for the Study of Trauma and Dissociation (www.isst-d.org). For further reading, consult some of the following references: Egner & Raz (2007); R. P. Kluft (1985, 1986, 1993c, 2012a); Lifshitz et al. (2012); and Raz, Fan, & Posner (2005).

Community Reintegration and Reconnection

At the outset of therapy, complex trauma clients are often isolated and life may focus primarily on management of symptoms and survival. This is not to say that there are no highly functioning persons with complex trauma, but this high functioning often comes at the price of enormous and exhausting effort. A dissociative client once spoke about all the switches of states she/he had to go through simply to get out of the house in the morning.

As one works through the traumatic experiences, it often happens that the person's life opens up. Therapy, which used to be the center of the client's universe, becomes less important. The client presents differently to others and often receives different interpersonal acceptance. Either spontaneously or through therapist suggestion and encouragement, the person begins to make more social connections. Often, in my experience, the client converts the trauma experience/narrative into a new life purpose. Survivors become church elders, Habitat for Humanity volunteers, elder care workers, and sometimes therapists themselves. The core story of having been harmed is reworked into a story of "now I will work to make the world a better place."

There begins to be a sense that one day therapy will end. The person will go forward in life, often with a renewed sense of mission or purpose, often without therapist help.

The issue then comes up of how to terminate the therapy without disturbing a healing relationship that has been central to resolution and growth. How to let go slowly? What, if any, relationship should be maintained? How cautious the termination? How not to leave the client feeling prematurely dismissed? How not to leave the client feeling held onto overlong? The third stage contains these delicate and crucial relationship management decisions. Clumsy handling can lead to damaging the work already accomplished. Competent and kind handling can yield a client sad and nostalgic, but ready to leave and functioning far better.

The next section of the book introduces some of the complex relational issues during the three-stage process. The relational crises described are certainly not exhaustive. From my experience gained in 40 years of work, and from the reactions of numerous therapists to whom I taught this model, the crises appear to be useful descriptions of regularly occurring choice points and their management. And they emphasize, again, the centrality of relationship in the work. Relationship without technique appears to result in merely supportive treatment. Technique without relationship often fails. Application of technique within a kind and bounded relationship is the key to deep and lasting change (P. Kinsler, 2015; P. J. Kinsler, 1992, 1995, 2014; P. J. Kinsler et al., 2009; R. P. Kluft, Kinsler, & O'Neil, 2014).

7

THE SIX CHOICE POINTS DEFINED

Stage One: Safety and Stabilization

The Opening Gambit

Entire books have been written about the so-called frame of therapy (Langs, 1980, 1984, 1992, 2004). I prefer to think about initial discussions with clients as the development of interpersonal contracts. These most often occur at the meta-level—broad and sometimes unfortunately unstated agreements about what will go on, and what the (often unconscious) structure of the relationship will be.

The way the client presents for therapy is the "opening gambit" in creation of the therapy structure—how the client wants to be seen and treated, and how he or she intends to see you. The opening gambit refers primarily to the client's interpersonal behaviors and patterns of behaviors, and the kinds of reactions these behaviors often bring from others. So, a highly clingy client may pull over-involvement from some persons/therapists and rejection and coldness from others. Therapists working from a relational crisis model will instead work on observing these patterns, the behaviors they pull from others, and then design a therapeutic approach *to give the client a different experience that can help them change.* So, for example, rather than either approach described previously for the dependent client, the therapist constructs a stance of gentle encouragement for the person to take and feel their own power and initiative.

Our initial discussions and negotiations make meta-relational statements as we craft agreements about:

1. Fees
2. Emergencies
3. Confidentiality
4. Medications
5. Hospitalization
6. The frequency and timing of therapy
7. What between-session work is expected
8. Whether we can validate or "discover" abuse memories
9. How we will deal with between-session written materials from clients
10. How we will deal with vacations, absences, and illnesses on both sides
11. Coverage for vacations and unanticipated events
12. Support animals, stuffed animals, non-patients in the sessions, dealing with the patient's family
13. Co-therapy with the patient's primary relationship if they are in such a relationship
14. Performing therapy for their partner too
15. If the partner is referred, what communications between therapists will be allowed
16. Discussion of the client's therapy in supervision/consultation
17. How we will work with the client's other providers—physicians, physical therapists, alternative healers, community or residential support persons, lawyers for the client, etc.
18. What circumstances, if any, will lead to a termination of the therapy

How we deal with these contracting steps determines the boundaries, safety, and predictability of the relationship. They are the floor or foundation upon which the rest of the therapy rests. Therapists come from varied professional backgrounds such as medicine, psychology, counseling, social work, etc. Many of these professional organizations have specific guidelines on the contracting steps just discussed, and often recommend provision of and discussion of these policy issues in writing, and obtaining informed consent from clients. See, for example, the recommendations of the American Psychological Association Ethical Principles (American Psychological Association, 2002, 2010; American Psychological Association Committee on the Revision of the Specialty Guidelines for Forensic Psychology, 2011). Other professional groups have similar documents, often available at the association's website. For example, social work ethics can be found at www.socialworkers. org/pubs/code/code.asp.[1]

Some of the crucial messages and potentially unconscious structural agreements negotiated at this stage are answers to unstated questions such as the following:

1. Will you take care of me like my parents didn't?
2. Can I have my dependency yearnings met? Constant hugs and reassurance?
3. Will you promise never to leave me?
4. Will you promise that any behavior I display will still lead to unconditional regard and/or love?
5. Can I scare you away with my angry parts?
6. Can I scare you away with my needy parts?
7. Will you never hurt me?
8. Will you never disappoint me?
9. Will you agree with how I perceive the world whether this is distorted or not?
10. Will you agree to believe that all my somatic symptoms are real and not psychologically based in whole or in part?

We discuss these relational "bids" in detail in Chapter 8, Opening Gambits.

The First Emergency

Complex trauma survivors frequently have emergencies. If complex trauma survivors don't ever display extensive needs or powerful emergent feelings, one had best look for therapist pleasing, "being a good patient," and viewing you as a potential abuser. The content of the first emergency is important. One always needs to deal with what is going on at the surface of the interaction. This varies from suicidality to family conflicts to relationship issues, work, or health complaints, etc. There is always a relational underlying question and this question is most often "Are you going to be able to help me? Will I overwhelm you or will you be able to cope?" "Can you safely contain my chaos?"

Typical therapist relational responses to emergencies range between "the fire engine," involving overwrought rescuing, and "the shipping container," involving over-rigid boundaries and lack of adequate involvement. The rescuing pole can set up a cycle of helplessness and inappropriate dependence in the client along the lines of "I'm so injured, you come and fix me." This stance can lead to years of testing and constantly seeking the therapist's unlimited attention and concern. It's exhausting for therapists, clients, and likely community resources as well.

An overly absent or rigid stance is also problematic. Complex trauma survivors are hyper-focused on relational indifference and rejection and a cold, distant, interpretive stance on the part of the therapist can be terrifying, and constantly stir up feelings of abandonment.

There's a middle ground between the two poles involving the therapist providing a safe container with limits.

So many presentations and trainings stop here, as if the therapy rolls along to fruition if we just get the beginning right. Getting the beginning right is a start, but it does not determine whether the therapy eventually will be a success. There are at least four other major "therapeutic rapids" that must be negotiated.

Stage Two: Working Through and Reassessing the Trauma

The Gestalt therapists reminded us to pay attention to the obvious. Two major sets of feelings are created by a lengthy history of child abuse, pain, and rage. A third corollary feeling that often overlays and prevents our getting to those two is shame.

Being ashamed of oneself protects the child from the hurt and rage; it turns off these feeling in childhood to preserve safety and attachments (J. J. Freyd, 1996; J. J. Freyd & Birrell, 2013).

The safe container of the relationship established during the first two major relational negotiations/crises *eventually gets taken in as an antidote to the shame*. As we give the client a new set of experiences in the therapy room, we can eventually aid them in diminishing the shame enough to allow the hurt and rage to emerge. It does not happen fast. A client once said that it is like one drop of honey sliding down her throat each session, making the insides just a tiny bit sweeter each time. As the shame abates, the hurt and rage emerge.

The Empty Depression

Too often, therapists and theorists use fancy words to describe basic human experiences. Narcissistic supplies. A secure base. Basic trust. These all point to a felt experience of being filled, through parental love and safety, with confidence and hope (J. Bowlby, 1980; Erikson, 1950; Kohut & Wolf, 1992). When a child is looked at with love and acceptance, happy things occur in the brain and the neurotransmitters (S. W. Porges, 1998). Without enough of those interactions a sense of emptiness and depletion and need and hurt and yearning often result for the child. As the therapy relationship aids the client in letting go of self-blame, this vast whirlwind of emptiness emerges. It is profound. Therapies get stuck both avoiding this "pit" and jumping into it without an escape plan. One of the core issues of the middle phase of therapy is walking the client through this pit and out the other side. This is where knowledge of rapid and deep trauma processing techniques is necessary. To use a metaphor from EMDR, the key is going through the trauma and out the other side (Shapiro, 2001). Many techniques exist to get this done; the core of the crisis is not to avoid it and successfully process it.

And once that is done, hopefully in this order, the next interpersonal challenge or crisis emerges—the destabilizing rage.

The Destabilizing Rage

When someone hurts us, we get angry. It is basic self-preservation. When someone is hurt over and over and can neither express it nor resolve it, several things can happen, from acting out to developing enormous stored-up rage. Most of us are afraid of our rage and its potential, and so much of it is somaticized as a result. Eventually, when our clients realize how much they have been betrayed, and the shame has diminished, and the hurt has been expressed, the rage hits. Most abused clients get to the point of understanding that they did not deserve the treatment they received, and their diminished shame and self-blame allow the anger to emerge. This, in turn, can be expressed in a couple of primary ways: self-compassion, a positive development, or less positive expressions of the anger. How can we avoid negative outcomes such as our patients getting stuck in the anger, harming themselves, harming others, or launching into vindictive actions that keep them embroiled with their abusers? How can we use the energy of the anger in positive ways and as a propellant towards a better life? If we are successful, the client can move towards reconnection with the external world phase of Stage 3.

Stage 3: Reconnection and Termination

Rebuilding a Life

Most of the chronic trauma clients I have worked with come to therapy with diminished or non-existent connections to others and to the world around them. They are isolated in their shame, or locked in relationships that reinforce their worthlessness. They may well be in relationships stuck in a very badly unconsciously negotiated opening gambit contract, along the lines of what was discussed earlier about the therapy relationship. One client had a "support person" who had "bought" the contract that he was never to disappoint his chronically traumatized friend—and so was at the client's beck and call for every disappointment, every medical provider who did not "understand," every birthday that no one made enough of a big deal about. This helper person was constantly being paid back, blamed, excoriated, for not doing "enough" for the survivor, despite what appeared to be monumental efforts, when judged by an outside observer.

In other cases, clients are so isolated that the therapy becomes the entire focus of their existence. Every moment between sessions—and being separated from the therapist—is excruciating. The therapy is their entire world. Many survivors believe there is no one out there for them and never will be, so they cling and become preoccupied with someone who interacts with and responds to them.

Once the grief has been processed and the rage expressed, there is often a vast sense of all that has been lost in life. The person is no longer traumatized, but is often bereft and alone. And, of course, deeply rejection phobic. The reconnection phase involves the building or rebuilding of human relationships.

The client's internal mantra should change from "no one will have me" to "maybe there are some safe people out there who will accept and become close to me." Of course, the therapy is designed to be the paradigm for the "safe enough" relationship. But that's not enough if the client is still not functional or involved with others. This phase is about helping the person take some interpersonal risks and build a life.

One example: For years Ms. X, highly educated but repeatedly sexually abused, insisted that "there are no men out there." No one to have a relationship with. No one who wouldn't use her. No one who wouldn't just use her for sex and then discard her. And as her conception of self changed, so did her perception of others. So, when she bumped into the chubby physics professor at a concert and they got to talking, she neither decided he would never have her, nor did she reject him because he wasn't conventionally "good-looking enough" for the likes of her. Although the building of trust between these two took a couple of years, they eventually merged their lives into a quite caring and companionable marriage.

Terminating the Relationship Without Destroying Its Work

A friend who is a wonderful baker maintains that no matter her efforts, her baked goods never come out looking like "the picture in the book." Often our therapies do not. Therapists are taught to process the loss of the relationship, set up solid boundaries about contact thereafter, end with a warm handshake, and be available should the client's life again require it. And sometimes it goes like this, and there is a mutually satisfying and sometimes softly nostalgic planned termination that goes well.

However, just like with teenagers leaving home, it doesn't all go smoothly. There are at least two other major patterns of termination that do not necessarily indicate failure.

The first of these is the "drifting away" pattern. The client, who has religiously kept twice a week appointments for years, through storm and flood, either suddenly starts missing, or, even better, calls you up with something better to do. What a victory that is!

One day an extraordinarily dutiful client called to cancel. There had never been any cancellations except for serious illness for years. This time the client called saying that he would be missing a session because he and a friend were going to the home show; there was some stuff he wanted to do to his house. Two victories—the client had a friend to go with, and something in his life was more important than therapy!

The more difficult pattern of termination is the "storming away" pattern. The client, who had previously been doing much better, begins to find fault, to blame, to again, as at the beginning of therapy, notice every tiny relational attunement miscue. And eventually he or she storms away angry and the therapist is left with bruised feelings.

Perhaps this is a self-comforting confabulation, but over the years I have noticed that, even in these therapies that seem to turn sad and bitter at the end, once the client has angrily hacked through the bonds between you, he or she has generally gone on to function better. I have told myself that this is similar to many teenagers needing to leave home by storming out. The anger fuels propulsion to the next stage of life.

Now let's look at the overall relational messages of the therapy, the meta-messages one hopes to send, and how this plays out over the course of the six crises.

Note

1. Retrieved 2/2/2017 from www.socialworkers.org

PART III
THE SIX CRISES IN DETAIL

8
THE OPENING GAMBIT

The Insecure/Ambivalent/Preoccupied Client

Have you ever gone into therapy? If so, try to remember why, and how that felt. Many people enter therapy when there is a threat of failure to a major relationship, but there may be many other sources of distress that cause them to seek help. The person's behaviors have often pushed some outside party to insist that "they need help." Can you remember filling out that first questionnaire in the waiting room? Wondering if the therapist was going to like you? If you could even have a prayer of explaining your coiled insides to another human being in depth? If they would hurt you, shame you, not care, or indicate by word or even slight shoulder shrug that your issues didn't matter? Or if they would rapidly blame you for whatever the current crisis was?

I certainly remember those fake Danish modern chairs, the plaid upholstery, the sterile walls of the Student Counseling Center, the furtive work of not meeting anyone else's eyes—all the while trying to figure out what those other people were there for. And being sure they were doing the same to me. I wondered if my shame was transparent, if someone would fix me with a look, leaving me even more mortified than when I walked in the door. If I might melt or curl up in a fetal position or run out, hiding my face.

If you've never been in therapy, find/download a copy of the movie *Ordinary People* and watch the scene where one of the young characters tries to decide to call for therapy. He finds a pay phone (it's an old

movie) where he can stare up at the therapist's office building. And dials
and hangs up and dials and hangs up.

Reaching out for therapy for most people is a very tentative, risk- and
shame-filled process. Although some may enter with false bravado, the
terror of exposure and abandonment and being found worthless under-
girds virtually everyone.

Now imagine what this situation is like for the complex trauma
survivor who has likely been mauled repeatedly by life over extended
time periods and most often in multiple ways: physical abuse, sexual
abuse, verbal abuse, abandonment, parental alcoholism, parental incarceration, domestic violence, child pornography or trafficking, and all
the possible combinations of these traumas. The choice for therapy is
often motivated not only by relational conflicts and dead-ends, but
also by debilitating depression and anxiety, suicidality, self-mutilation,
addictive collapse, repeated revolving-door hospitalizations, and/or
the inability to function in a work setting. What does it take to pick up
that phone? To make the appointment? To even give a brief description to secretarial staff or voice mail or some impersonal intake form
on a tablet? Can you feel how risky it is? How in so many respects it
feels like and may indeed be a life or death situation? In my experience, most of the clients who have come in have done so at the point
of immediate crisis or imminent life collapse. And now we want them
to talk to us.

Although some clients may come in presenting differently on the
surface, particularly those in the insecure/dismissive attachment stance,
who present as armored and without needs, the underlying terror of
mortification or annihilation by others, including the therapist, is still
there. *So, our clients present with unspoken interpersonal contracts unconsciously designed to create a relationship that will not shatter them further.*
Our sensitivity to what is being asked in these initial contracting steps
can create functional or dysfunctional therapeutic agreements that neither party has made conscious to him/herself or spoken aloud about to
each other.

*Most often the unconscious contract "offered" us by the client is the very one
that has worked so poorly in the non-therapy world.*

When I worked in suicide prevention center volunteer-training programs, and later in other therapist teaching assignments, we used the following exercise to illustrate this point. Picture two chairs facing each other. The therapist is seated on one chair, the client facing them on the other. Now add in two other parties, standing behind each chair, the therapist's alter ego and the client's. The job of the alter ego is to state out loud that which is not said in the therapist/client conversation.

So, for example:

Client (CL): Hi, nice to meet you.
Client alter ego (CAE): She looks creepy; hope she doesn't hurt me.
Therapist (Tx): Nice to meet you too. . .
Therapist Alter Ego (TxAE): Oh dear, she looks so fragile; hope this isn't a draining one.

The unconscious interpersonal contracting is done between the client alter ego (CAE) and the therapist alter ego (TxAE).

In the best and most consciously negotiated opening gambit arrangements, these unstated fears, attributions, and assumptions are surfaced and made a part of the discussion; this leads to therapist-patient agreements with less chance of eventual entrapment and stagnation or collapse.

Here is an example from a training workshop entitled "Words Matter" that I conducted with two colleagues, Joan Turkus and Kathy Steele, to illustrate how therapists actually speak to clients, in negotiating these opening gambits and attempting not to fall into previously damaging relational stances. The following is an instance of such a negotiation with an insecure/ambivalent/preoccupied client (P. Kinsler, Turkus, & Steele, 2015):

C: You'll come to visit me in the hospital like my last therapist did, right?
TxAE: Oy!
Tx: Can you tell me any more about that?
TxAE: Better stall for time while I figure this one out . . .

C: Well, I was in the hospital seven times last year and every time up until the last my therapist came to visit me. Then she just sort of up and disappeared! I was heartbroken!

TxAE: Oy.

Tx: I wonder if you might feel better if you did not have to go into the hospital so often?

C: Oh no, I like it there. They're very nice to me, and I don't have to do things like cook and clean for myself.

TxAE: OK, I better find some way to make a connection with some part of this person that doesn't just yearn to be taken care of.

Tx: It sounds like you often feel like you need to be protected and taken care of.

C: Oh yes, absolutely.

Tx: I wonder if there were some things in your life that left you feeling that need?

C: Oh yes, my family was mean.

Tx: Do you think we might talk about that and see if we can help you get strong enough to not need the hospital so much?

C: Do you mean you won't visit me? Will you just put me there and dump me like the last ones?

TxAE: Oh dear . . .

Tx: I get that you've been let down a bunch in your life and have a lot of need to be cared for carefully.

C: Oh yes.

Tx: How about we see if we can help you gain enough strength to not need the hospital so often, and we make a decision about hospital visits if you have to go in? I think you would feel better if you gained strength on the outside.

C: Well, I could try . . .

Here, the therapist has not acceded to a contract to meet the client's unmet dependency needs. This is not possible to do, actually. The therapist can be much more caring, dependable, safe, and predictable than the home environment. But he or she cannot fill a bucket with holes. Here the therapist has, hopefully gently, stated that the contract will not be one of re-parenting and filling the bucket, but will instead be one of strengthening the client's coping and self-reliance abilities. And hopefully this has and can be done in a way that feels respectful, and like the client is with someone who has walked this path before, enormously reassuring to frightened and fragile clients. Letting go of the dependency needs will require a grieving and angering process when the client is strong enough to do so, combined with a letting go of these unmet needs.

Understanding Dependency

Why do so many survivors of severe abuse lead with dependency and wishes to be re-parented? Children raised in the insecure/ambivalent/preoccupied attachment matrix are subject to a universally felt human need to complete a "gestalt," a whole experience rather than a partial one. Whether it is visual figures or human relationships, we do not like things incomplete (Wikipedia, 2016, URL: https://en.wikipedia.org/wiki/Principles_of_grouping).

My observation of clients over many years—and often of their marital/primary relationship choices—shows that people often choose persons very similar to those they have had conflictual relationships with in the past. Whether we call this repetition compulsion or something else, human beings seem to almost fasten onto the lapels of people who are similarly depriving as those in their home environments, and then to wish to "shake them into doing right by them."

Once, I saw a client who had remarried the same alcoholic man twice despite his cheating on her and getting thrown out of his profession for misconduct. And when, after years of therapy, she came to finally let him go, she again chose boyfriends who were demeaning, disparaging, distant, and difficult. This client had always been rather defensive about exploring the relationship with her father, until said man was on his deathbed. There was then a gestalt-completing conversation in which the father apologized for the horrors his years of alcoholism and neglect had imposed on this client. A little while later, in therapy, she could finally cry about what she had not gotten from her father, and to review his attempted amends-making, which she was letting in drop by drop.

We then got to discussing her then-current alcoholic boyfriend. He was relatively new so I asked more about him. The client replied with perhaps the best metaphor I have heard to describe this lapel-shaking phenomenon. She said the new boyfriend was "same cake, different icing." She had identified her repeated attempts to re-do the early family gestalt by getting a similar man to turn around and "love her right." And as she worked through the loss of her now deceased father, she also let go of the current boyfriend and took a significant amount of time working on herself and grieving before engaging in another love relationship, this time with a different type.

Object-relations therapists call this the "desirable deserter" phenomenon (Guntrip, 1973), referring to the repeat pattern of engaging with tempting but withholding and withdrawing persons, who consistently disappear over the horizon and disappoint. This pattern tends to recur until it is identified and profound grief and letting go occur. And therapists must become comfortable witnessing and participating in this grief process. Human beings change in a variety of ways, from changed thoughts to worked-through emotions. Among the most powerful changes are the ones achieved by the grieving and letting-go process. Trauma therapists must become comfortable witnessing and facilitating this process.

Laurie's Opening Gambits

I described Laurie in an earlier chapter, in discussing how we quickly size up and make assumptions about clients. Here and in subsequent chapters we follow Laurie over the course of the six choice points as one paradigmatic example of an insecure/ambivalent/preoccupied client. Unfortunately, treating her involved many "beginner mistakes," requiring me to learn by experience and to seek outside consultation and training from experts in the field of complex trauma and dissociation. The chaos of Laurie's initial treatment and Laurie herself caused me to observe the many relational mistakes I made as I learned more and developed the relational crisis model we are discussing.

What I primarily failed to do initially with Laurie was to set up a secure structure with many of the pre-treatment arrangements explicitly worked out. It was not till years later that I learned of the pre-treatment contracting triangle (J. Turkus & Kinsler, 2014).

So, I did negotiate fees as this was an insurance case, and I did make a firm commitment to fight for what she needed from insurance. I did not negotiate emergencies, taking the false heroic stance that I would "manage" them and not anticipating them as a problem. (Boy, did I learn.) I think my boundaries about confidentiality towards her family members were not explicit. I made no formal arrangements about what would lead to hospitalization. I made no demands about her doing therapy work between sessions. I did not anticipate receiving a lot of between-session materials and so did not discuss them until they came flooding in. I did not set up how emergencies would be handled on vacations other than by calling my pager, until much later in the therapy. I was muddy about whether I could/would help the husband or the children either individually or in family work. I was not explicit on how I would use consultation or supervision. I took it as a matter of course that I would coordinate her medications with her psychiatric provider without assessing what level of cooperation or competition or condescension I might receive. I did not anticipate that there might be any thought of suing her prior abusers or confronting them with or without my help. I never discussed if and how either of us might end the therapy, either through blow-ups on either side or successful termination.

Given the lack of structure that I provided at the time, this therapy could have been (should have been?) a disaster. Instead, it was eventually a real success. However, had I known then to pay attention to some of the 18 opening gambit setup questions discussed in Chapter 6, the therapy could have been safer, shorter, less chaotic, and less stressful for both of us. This is the therapy behind much of the relational thinking in this book. Because what did work was *an absolutely overarching commitment to try to understand what was happening inside Laurie and in our therapy relationship, and to then try to discuss and process it.* And as we did so, we both made needed course corrections that made the work safer, deeper, and more productive. In this particular therapy, the relational commitment prevented the collapse of a badly structured therapy provided by a newbie to complex trauma therapy. I believe it was the strength of the relationship between us and our mutual perseverance that eventually made the mistakes salvageable.

The Pre-Treatment Triangle of Choices for Safety

If I were to re-do this opening gambit phase, I would use, and have since used, the pre-treatment contracting triangle taught me by Joan Turkus. Note that this is "a plan and not a promise." It is a set of discussions with the client that provides practical choices, but also sends the interpersonal message that the client needs to work in collaboration with the therapist towards a secure base within the therapy. It sends the message that the client is still responsible for his or her life, but the therapist will aid the client in developing a safe structure to do the work within secure boundaries (J. Turkus, 2014).

Picture a pyramid with the point facing down, so that it narrows towards the base. Now picture drawing five lines across the triangle. This produces a triangle divided into five stripes, if you will. Each stripe is a step in the safety planning triangle.

Step one is things the client can do on his/her own. This "stripe" should be discussed and developed in partnership with the client and consist of as many choices as possible. For example, if the client is dysregulated and/or suicidal, they could listen to soothing music, take a shower, take a walk, do breathing exercises, work out, draw, write in a journal, use an adult coloring book, etc. With the client, develop as many of these as possible. These are the first steps the client should/can take in dealing with dysregulation and upset.

Step two should involve six to ten choices centered on drawing in supports available to the client. Such steps could include things such as visiting a religious institution, going to an AA meeting, asking a friend to come over, or engaging in a favorite activity.

Step three involves more active asking for help such as calling a crisis hotline, visiting a support center for persons with mental illness, or requesting a new appointment with the therapist closer in time. If possible, this step should include three to five choices.

Step four involves actively seeking professional help such as calling the therapist's crisis number or pager, asking for an immediate visit from a crisis team, or going to a local emergency room.

The final step in the triangle is rapidly instituting hospitalization to ensure safety.

Collaborating on development of such a triangle provides comfort and reassurance to both client and therapist, and is also a good example of the therapist working with the client and thereby delivering a message that the client's planning and thought processes are valued and respected. This is an important message in counteracting the powerlessness often felt by the complex trauma survivor.

Insecure/ambivalent/preoccupied clients such as Laurie require and deserve a much safer container than I could provide at the beginning of this therapy, and the therapy got better as we *gently* renegotiated the initial mess. A lot of this renegotiating occurred during the handling of emergencies, which is discussed in the next chapter.

The Insecure/Dismissive Client's Opening Gambit

As discussed previously, insecure/dismissive clients hope for connection but have felt "burned" and let down so often in their early childhood that they develop armor and act as if they do not need anything from others.

Special assistant to the chief of the medical center, Roberta was a well-recognized, queen-like figure at the hospital. Rumor had it she was the one who ran the place, regularly making corporate vice presidents feel like scolded schoolchildren.

She strode through the corridors with a sense of ownership, head high, shoulders back. Clothing was professional, perfect, even if a little too tight. One could not fault it, but it caught the eye. There was a zone around her. Somehow you knew not to get too close to that space, to always stand an inch or two farther back than one might talking to another. Every request was filled professionally and dutifully, yet, when dealing with her, one always had the sense of danger, of how easy it might be to go over some invisible line that could provoke an enormously clever put-down or maybe even an explosion. You had the sense you had better not mess.

So, I was enormously surprised when she asked for an appointment, and was out there in my waiting room. It turned out she had been watching me for quite some time in the halls as I went about my business, finding my awkward shyness "cute" and non-threatening. She noted how I treated the people who came to see me, watching the brief hallway or waiting room greetings. Always sizing up whether I dealt with people with respect, and still carried enough personal authority that I might be of use to her.

So, the opening gambit here took place over the course of weeks to months, and I was not really aware of it. Roberta was sizing me up from the insecure/dismissive stance. Was I worth her time? Could I respect the powerful exterior while looking beneath gently?

The initial therapy request was whether I could help her "shape up" a boyfriend of "high potential" who was an engineering whiz but who was unable to reliably devote his attention to her. He made but did not carry out promises. She described him as behaving like one of those gag coffee cups: "If a man says he will do something, he will. No need to remind him every six months or so!"

Initially, Roberta treated me with humorous scorn, as if she couldn't believe she was going to someone like me for help. As if the cheerleading queen was somehow going out with the science nerd. This frame of the therapist being one-down on the social desirability scale was very difficult for me to deal with. It required not allowing the one-down power probes to grab my inner insecure high school kid; in other words, to not play into the "I'm way above you, deigning to speak to you" stance, with which she approached the world.

It took months of not responding defensively to the barbs before she was safe enough to talk about how that way of acting protected her. I made rare attempts to point out these interpersonal operations, when I thought she might be able to hear them, only to be greeted by derisive laughter or a scornful face. She was not ready.

Roberta had learned to use her smarts and her conventionally sexually attractive appearance to keep people at bay. Why had she done so?

When we could get an overarching view of her interpersonal operations, as if watching her behavior and interactions from the top of a hill (often called a *meta-perspective*), we learned that she had been sexually abused by a stepfather over many years. Her mother was dominated by this man, who controlled all finances, where the family lived, and the kind of work the entire family was involved in. He had a modus operandi of purchasing a business that required everyone in the family to help run the operations. The "family business" kept Roberta, her brothers and sisters, and her mother under constant observation, supervision, and control. If one of the children stepped out of line (or he perceived that they did), he beat them. Her mother did not try to intercede; she simply looked away. The mother had no vocational skills. She had six kids. She was not about to rock the boat. And she used the very strong tenets of her church to not even think about divorce.

There was no "breakthrough moment" in the therapy. I listened and did not judge or intrude, but I *was* very attentive to her discussions about her boyfriend and her deep sense of not getting what she wanted. And I was able eventually to point out her keeping me away by funny put-downs or "revelations" about how other people at the hospital viewed me.

There is something of the "art" of therapy here that is hard to convey in words. Let's for a moment talk about it as an inner wise-mind therapist: the organic integrative listener and weaver who hears and observes all those many layers of interaction discussed at the beginning of this book, and either gives the "go" signal to intervene, to make a statement, or does not. When I had listened respectfully "enough," had not retaliated against the funny put-downs, had not hung my head in shame either, but had been able to laugh at myself, had joined her in seeing parts of myself as funny, there was a melting. The barriers to talking about her ways of interacting with others dropped. It was finally time to say something about all the clever ways she kept me away and on my toes.

And that's when I learned about the extremely sharp surgical scalpel she kept in her purse, and her knowledge of how to quickly and fatally use it on herself. And about the spider silk–thin thread that prevented her from using that scalpel. And that's when she made a powerful attachment to therapy that enabled years of work on the intense traumas that made her staying alive such a moment-to-moment, poised-at-the-precipice, risky business.

But we couldn't get there until a moment occurred of her saying a teasing something when I could point out how she used that interpersonal operation to maintain distance and safety. My memory is that we had been working together long enough for us to laugh together when we could surface that operation and she could—mostly—drop it. The stance was respectful distance, but with confidence in the therapeutic method and gentle probing. A supervisor once told me that the way one worked with defensive clients was not by bashing down the door, but by searching around the locked house for a window that had been left open a crack. We found that window in a mutual ability to laugh at ourselves without the humor being a barb that provoked shame. My thought process went something like this: "What can this client hear where we can be unguarded for a moment?"

The Disorganized Attachment Client's Opening Gambit

To review, this kind of client has found no successful way to obtain safe attachment and calming of fear in childhood, and their attachment behaviors are regularly incoherent, disorganized, and "all over the place." The following is a discussion of the opening gambit with one such man:

Frank was all over the map—literally—job to job, woman to woman, one substance abuse treatment program to another. Dangerously, he was a long-haul trucker with an unpredictable schedule, and substance problems severe enough to make him a menace. And, of course, his wife sent him in—she knew about the affairs, the drinking and the pills, but they had kids and as so often was true, "When he wasn't drinking he was a great guy." It was hard to pin him to a therapy schedule. He was in this part of the country, then that. A trip to California would come up, then one down the East Coast. He was like one of those wooden paddles with a ball and elastic band attached. Spring off in one direction, "sprong" off in another. His life could not, did not, sit still. His long-suffering wife, who improbably believed he was "salvageable," sometimes corralled him into keeping appointments. She also encouraged him into a job that involved more local driving during weekdays, so there might be some stability at home, and to the therapy.

He was an unwanted child, the eighth in line from a Catholic family with an alcoholic father who worked as a laborer. There was never enough money, food, clothing. He was routinely passed off to one or another older sister as their responsibility. In some large families, the older siblings are bedrock, acting kindly as surrogate parent figures and aiding in establishing some safe structure. Not so in this one. Brothers abused drugs; sisters had substance-using boyfriends; the littlest child was often ignored and routinely sexually abused. He started his own drinking at age 8. Smoked the roaches of marijuana cigarettes after the brothers and sisters partied. He was always good with his hands, with fixing things or taking them apart, to see how they worked. Dropped out of high school at age 16, the first day he could. But it didn't matter as he soon parlayed his Mr. Goodwrench side into a job at a small engine repair place. Eventually, he even started his own small-engine and landscaping-machine repair business, but he drank and pill-popped it away, along with his first wife and their two kids.

Nothing changed until I pointed out to him that the chaos was a great way to run from his feelings, and to show me on the outside how he was feeling on the inside. Although the chaos never completely subsided, he *was* able to get that job just trucking through New England and to be home nights. Later he was able to re-open his business. He began to make two out of three and then three out of four therapy sessions. He began to talk about how nobody ever wanted him or needed him to be alive, and that the womanizing felt good because it momentarily made him feel wanted, desired, worthy. We return to Frank's therapy over the remainder of the book, and track his movement through the six crises.

What was the "opening gambit" stance that allowed Frank to settle in? Although, of course, I would like to ascribe it to my therapeutic brilliance, the truth was his wife's steadiness and belief were crucial. She saw the devastated boy inside, loved him (but not his behavior), and kept trying to bring him to safe pasture. Later, Frank told me that actually feeling loved inside began to melt the need to run and churn. My therapeutic stance was one of steadiness with predictability and containment. I kept the same time open even as he routinely tried to switch appointments. I repeatedly told him I would be there but could not and would not have my schedule disrupted by his every chaos-crisis. I focused phone calls back into session time. I brought the wife in at times, for steadiness and support. I did not chase him around or try to rescue him. Rescuing usually results in the disorganized client's running faster. What also did not happen was scorning and blaming—he'd had plenty of that. The productive stance was "I'm here when you are ready to settle down and do some work." I assume there would have been a time when I would/could have given up on him. However, the steadiness drew him in: "There's something that can help you here if you slow down enough to learn from it."

The Opening Gambit—Summary and Takeaway Points

1. The initial ways a person approaches therapy, their interpersonal operations, are clues to their attachment style.
2. How we feel inside is an important clue to the client's interpersonal operations.
    a. Insecure/ambivalent/preoccupied clients often present with intense dependency needs and we feel either like rescuing or pushing away, depending on our own level of comfort with dependency.
    b. Insecure/dismissive clients keep us at arms-length and present with an armor that takes time and patience and just the right balance between pushing and respecting, till the person's facade begins to "melt."
    c. Insecure/disorganized clients present with chaos, and our task is to find the eye of the hurricane long enough to pull the person to some stable center.
3. It is typical that the work of change can only begin in depth when the initial opening gambit presentation is made conscious to the client and ourselves, and we then look underneath for familial causes.
4. When the gambit is identified, often a literal or figurative deep sighing occurs in the relationship, and the client feels seen and understood. Our experience here is that we have moved from a therapy

that feels tentative, in which communication misunderstandings are always a danger, to a safer working alliance in which the client is ready to do the work of therapy. Forming a good working alliance leads to a sense within the therapist that "we are on the same page," allies working together on the problems and symptoms.

5. The experience of being seen and understood and cared about is in itself healing. How often do human beings have the experience of someone caring enough to work at deeply understanding them?

    a. However, empathy alone does not cure. It is a necessary but not sufficient condition. It sets the groundwork for the eventual working through of trauma. It is not enough by itself (R. P. Kluft, Kinsler, & O'Neil, 2014). One of the major failings I have seen in years of training therapists is the application of empathy without direction. Empathy allows deeper probing and resolution of the wounds but is not curative in itself. It can result in a therapy that can be characterized as taking an "oh, you poor dear" position without any knowledge of how to move beyond the legacy of trauma.

9
THE FIRST CRISIS/EMERGENCY

As discussed previously, complex trauma clients typically make emergency contacts, unless they are working hard as therapist pleasers and viewing you as a potential abuser. And, of course, there is content in a first crisis. Something sets off a crisis or an emergency. Our clients have repetitive problems with emotional dysregulation. They have multiple triggers. Any one, or a combination of triggers can provoke the first crisis contact. For those new to complex trauma therapy, the following are some of the potential triggers for crises:

1. Outside stimuli that are similar to traumatizing events. The classic example is the July 4th fireworks taken for incoming shelling by the traumatized veteran. But it can be varied kinds of outside stimuli—sounds, the physical configuration of a space, tones of voice, conversations about sensitive topics. Whatever the stimulus, it pushes the "play" button on the stored fear responses in the client's limbic system.
2. Somatic triggers such as bodily feelings or memories arising without the attached context.
3. Anniversary reaction to a particular time of the year during which traumatizing events happened. Halloween reactions, reactions to the time of summer camp, and reactions to specific holidays all fit here.
4. Interpersonal relationship triggers: Our clients are especially sensitive to changes in the status of relationships, and these can be both positive and negative changes. Coldness/withdrawal of a love

object is often extremely provoking, throwing the client back to the time when there was no consistent attachment, with the same panic that we have seen in the insecurely attached infant. But increases in warm feelings can also provoke a crisis. I have seen a client enter therapy because, after being frozen in the insecure/dismissive position, they began to feel loved by a partner who stood by them for many years. The feelings of being loved began to penetrate, and the client became terrified.

Whatever the content of the crisis, there is also a relational process within the therapy. The crisis poses a series of questions for the therapist-client relationship:

1. Will you be there for me outside of the normal hours of business? Do I matter enough?
2. Can you actually aid me to feel safe when I am completely panicked? Can you help me return to a state of reasonable, manageable calm?
3. Can the parts of me that know I do not deserve any thoughtful holding get you to abandon me like everyone else? Indeed, I am expecting to be left alone with my pain, and I know many ways of coping, which present the illusion of control. What can *you* provide that is more satisfactory than cutting, drinking, sexual acting out, hurting others? All these things have kept me alive, after all.
4. Can I blow you away with the extent of my pain? Is this something that you can imagine feeling? Will it destroy you? After all, I destroyed my parents and many lovers because of how hateful I am.
5. Can I blow you away with my rage? You've never seen rage like mine. I can devour the earth like one of those monsters in the video games that spits fire and shoots death rays through my arms. Do you really want to stand in the way of the death rays? You better get out while the getting's good. I've destroyed better therapists than you!
6. Well, if you *can* understand my pain and my collapse and my dysregulation, then will you be my Mommy? I always wanted a Mommy like you!

7. Well, if you *can* understand my sorrow, will you be the Daddy I never had? Do I have to do all those sex things to keep you here? I'm very good at them! Want to see?
8. I'll bet my chaos can drive you nuts. Just let me show you how chaotic life can be! I'll make you feel just what it was like when I was a kid having to take care of Mom while she drugged, and have sex with Daddy so he'd give us the money for food.
9. Watch me spin! You fix it!
10. I've had this loaded gun in my desk drawer since I was 14. Have you got anything to make me want to give it up? Well then, can I give it to you?

Any therapist working with complex trauma can likely add to the foregoing list. Is there a commonality that we can learn from in the relational meaning of the client's first crisis, however presented?

My experience has been that the first crisis most often asks the therapeutic question: *What kind of container are you going to be?* Although it is an eventual goal to work the client towards a collaborative model in which the power is shared, this is rarely available at the beginning of treatment. First, the client needs to feel intensely that they are in a safe-enough place. Although parenting analogies can be dangerous and taken too far, I want to draw an analogy to an infantile state of feeling. On the wall in my office there is a photograph of me holding my then 6-month-old grandson. He has virtually melted into my skin and fallen asleep, and I have partaken of the feeling of safety and psychological momentary melding—my head has nodded forward and I have fallen asleep with him. And, while sleeping, I am gently patting his back.

This is not something to *do* with a client, nor is it the position that the entire therapy should occupy. We cannot give clients a new past or a new better Mommy or Daddy. We can strive at the beginning to provide an atmosphere where the feeling that possibly, maybe a little, perhaps the client could, be safe enough to let his or her guard down. A set of responses to the question of what kind of container will you be whose answer is "safe enough." Winnicott talked about the "good enough mother" (Winnicott, 1969). Here, I am talking about "the safe enough therapist."

The Types of Containers and Their Consequences

Likely, many of us began our careers motivated to act like a trusty, dependable fire engine. At least, many of us did, myself included. It felt good to believe I could be a rescuer just like those other professionals I admired: policemen, firemen, and "real doctors" (MDs). Now, when I aid in training psychiatry residents, we discuss those who are "shepherds" and those who are not. The shepherds want to be deeply involved with the patient, follow them for very long periods, and perhaps "lead them to health" or at least better functioning. The non-shepherds just want to deliver a service. I was raised in the time when shepherding was seen as a core of the therapist's activity.

Psychologists Wilson and Lindy (1994) have provided a good model for understanding our personal countertransference stance regarding the relationships we form with complex trauma clients (Figure 9.1). According to their model, therapists vary on two

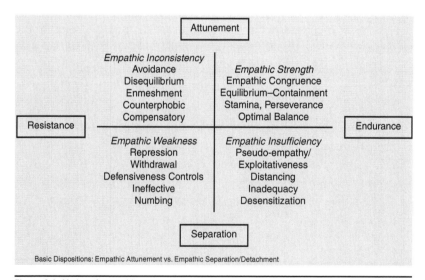

Figure 9.1 Modes of empathic attunement
© John P. Wilson and Jacob D. Lindy, 2002.

poles, between attunement and separation on one pole, and resistance and endurance on the other. When we are tuned in but resistant to the extent of the client's pain, we display empathic inconsistency. We are drawn in by the attunement and pull back out as a result of our resistance to feeling what the client feels.

Therapists who are attuned with high endurance can show continued empathic strength with "optimal balance." Therapists who are high in resistance with strong needs for separation show empathic weakness and often withdraw from or are numb to their client's pain. Therapists high in endurance but with very strong separation needs have insufficient empathy and provide "pseudo-empathy" or can even become exploitive.

I like to think of the various container styles with visual metaphors:

1. The shipping container metaphor:
    Therapists who are trained in primarily blank-screen therapeutic methods, and who have not adjusted to the special rejection sensitivities of the complex trauma patient, are often perceived by the client as similar to a closed and locked shipping container. Therapists who only interpret, and/or who respond very little, are perceived as cold and rejecting. Although many psychoanalytically trained therapists provide excellent care for trauma survivors, this often requires a flexibility, warmth, and connection that did not characterize the standard "psychiatrist behind the couch saying little" method.

    The shipping container metaphor captures the essence of the relational stance of the separated and resistant therapist.

    I once attended a weeklong therapist training workshop that offered instruction in trauma therapies. At these events, one is often drawn into conversations with people not well known, around hastily arranged dinner tables or receptions or other conference events. I didn't know too many people in the trauma treatment community back then, and was seated with people who were new to me. We were talking about the workshop when one hearty-looking bearded fellow pronounced, "Well, if they can't be fun, I just don't treat them! Document two violations of the treatment contract and refer!" This was not a person to be found again at the many other years of trauma conferences I have attended. The empathic insufficiency and empathic weakness he displayed offer a glaring example of the shipping container style.

The thought patterns underlying this style are not the problem. As noted in the beginning of this book, transference, resistance, the importance of child development, and observing intrapsychic and interpersonal process all began in psychoanalytic theory and provide useful tools today.

The issue is using these tools in a warmer and more connected style than it is possible to do from a shipping container.

2. The broken vessel

The horror that human beings can inflict on each other within families is endless. Add natural disasters to that: famine, war, genocide—there is no limit. It is possible to feel it too deeply, to resonate so much to the client's pain that you as a therapist break or appear broken to the client. I once knew a therapist who cried every time a client discussed difficult emotions and traumatic experiences. Well, the client knew the therapist was feeling with him/her. But the client didn't know whether the therapist *knew a way out and through*. The client felt that she and the therapist were in the same boat, and neither of them knew how to steer.

For this type of therapist, a personal therapy is strongly urged. One needs to know the path, to have felt personal pain and grief, and to come out on the other side. When one has changed as the result of personal therapy, one has a deeply felt knowledge of what the effective therapist did for you—what was the combination of empathy, directedness, grief work, providing a new relational experience that *helped you change*? This will likely be a good place to start. Although initially the style you develop will most likely work best with people like you, over the years one expands that to other personality styles and presenting problems.

3. The commode

Persons who have been routinely abused have had abusers as models of behavior. They know how to abuse, how to transfer their anger to you, or dump their anger on you. And they unconsciously test whether you are any better at not getting dumped on than they were. All of which makes the toilet an apt, if uncomfortable, metaphor. We don't have to be the toilet. This is one of the places where firmness is called for: "I know you're very angry and sometimes wrist slashing and head banging get the feeling out—as does yelling at me. But I think you're really trying to tell me something about how you were made to feel as a child. And it is not OK to abuse yourself or others, including me."

4. The safe container

Picture a sink. One of those newer ones that sit atop the counter, shaped like a sculptural vessel. With sides that hold yet allow some splashing around, if you will. Not too tight and not too loose. Able to catch the splashes without letting them run all over. But some room to play. Be this sink!

Although this is, of course, facetious, it tries to express something that is hard to capture in words. The internal question for the therapist is what boundaries will make this client feel safer, more contained, without feeling crowded, or without walls, or, indeed, like they are going to go down the drain? (sorry, couldn't help it). But there is an internal sense of balance one can get if we keep asking the internal questions: Too tight? Too loose? Too disconnected and discarding? Too fuzzy? You have it right when there is that sigh in the room or on the phone, where the person feels heard and the gas goes out of the emergency dirigible.

The Insecure/Ambivalent/Preoccupied Client

Here's how it went with Laurie, our insecure/ambivalent/preoccupied client:

It must have been the fourth time the pager went off that weekend with a call from Laurie or about Laurie. Somehow that person had a way of dramatic emergencies that could get the community in arms, and also embarrass the treating therapist. This time she made a suicide attempt by flipping her car over in the river that ran behind our local hospital, where I was on staff, and everyone knew I took the "difficult-to-treat trauma patients." After they pried her out with the Jaws of Life and cleaned her up, and medically cleared her, and sent her to the psych ward, they put her on the phone with me. I was exasperated. I must admit to feeling stupid that my patient had done this in front of all my colleagues, when I was supposed to be "such an expert." I was tired from her other phone calls, from having two young children, from having a life. My temper was sitting there on my shoulder wanting to say something that would have blown up the therapy in a hurry. There's an internal fight that goes on when one is struggling with the first, initial countertransference reaction, between acting on it without noticing, and observing and catching it. It is a good habit to get into a conscious pattern of asking, "Is this about me? Is what I'm feeling going to move the therapy forward? Can I look at what's going on between us as another way of understanding the client and our relationship?" These are not our common reactions to our feelings, but they should become therapeutic habits. Our wise-mind therapist says, "What is this about? How might it be used? What's the danger if I just react?" As this becomes habit, it also can become fast.

As I was about to open my cranky mouth, "wise-mind therapist" popped up in that internal soft but strong voice asking whether this embarrassing dramatic suicide attempt was a test. Could Laurie blow me away? Could she scare me off? Would I retaliate? Would I dump her? She was unconsciously proposing these tests of my stability and the safety of the therapy. I caught my reactive mind just in time and instead of reacting posed a question.

My favorite questions in therapy often begin with "I wonder. . . ?" This grabs the observing part of the client, working with me to understand. I said something like, "Laurie, I wonder if this is a test? I wonder if you're trying to find out if you can push me away or get me to give up on you?" Remember, her last therapist had rather unceremoniously dumped her.

There was an audible two- or three-beat rest, as in a musical piece. The sobbing and the rage and the self-hate quieted for a moment and there was a breath. Her "observing part" had its curiosity peaked, and there was a feeling of both of us getting a tentative understanding of what had transpired. There was a palpable softening, as if the crisis had gone from a ten to a four in severity, and even a bit of a chuckle on Laurie's end on having been "found out," but responded to with compassion and not contempt or anger.

I would learn over time that Laurie had dissociative identity disorder, and this was certainly not the last test that her system of alter personalities posed for me; there were years of others—but we always had the paradigmatic example that I would not retaliate, that we could think it through together, that the meanings of the behavior were understandable, and that when those meanings were identified and talked about, the necessity for acting out diminished. This stood us well through years of trauma therapy and grief and anger work.

The Dismissive Client

What of crises for the dismissive client? I mentioned before that Roberta had a very passive-aggressive partner who continually promised without delivering. She was also pulled repeatedly into her enmeshed family, especially when her abusive stepfather was coming down regularly on her mother. And she had the invulnerable appearance at the hospital to maintain. Even for her, at one point all the pressures became too much and she came fuming into the office: "Why shouldn't I just kill myself?? That SOB does nothing around the house. My stepfather is all over my mother. She's calling all the time. My boss is an a-hole and insists I do all his work and I never get credit or promotions. I just got the same raise as everyone else after years of promises for an upgrade of my position. And all night long I'm having those dreams again! YOU tell me why I should even bother!" And again, she alluded to the scalpel in her purse, the insurance policy she maintained for when it just got too bad.

Parenthetically, the internal "marriage" to the idea of suicide is often a paradoxical lifesaver for clients like this. "Well, if it gets any worse, I can just . . ." It makes this moment tolerable because there is a potential way out.

In this case, letting Roberta fume was a catalyst. I did not try to talk her out of killing herself. I managed to hold off my savior therapist self and avoided giving a hundred possible solutions for her problems. I didn't generate plans with her for either her parents or her partner or her boss. I noted that this was one of the first times I had seen her out of control and mentioned what a relief it must be to just blow it off.

That did not do the trick, actually. She turned on me about making a therapist's inane comment, a stock phrase. She was momentarily scornful. "That's not enough! Blah blah how hard it must be. Boo hoo! Crap!"

What a lovely opportunity for me to get defensive and retaliate. I managed not to. I tried to insist that I was really hearing how overwhelmed she was and how I appreciated her telling me. There was a brief flicker of that getting in before the inevitable fight-back: "Huh! What do you know about it? Living in that nice country house with the nice wife and the two kids. Hah!" (There are very few secrets in small-town rural practice, where one is one of the few known psychotherapists).

I distinctly remember saying "that scalpel and your attachment to it scares me." She was standing now and still striding angrily around the room. She was at an angle to me and her head snapped back over her shoulder to make eye contact. She slowed her walk and went over to the couch and sat down. It was a moment of being real with her in a way that therapists often are not with clients, and that being real creates, enhances, improves the therapeutic alliance (C. Dalenberg, 2014; C. J. Dalenberg, 2004). I wish I could say that all this was in my mind when I told Roberta I was scared of her slashing her throat right there, right then, in my office. Other than as deep background, it was not what was in my mind. Hoping she wasn't going to kill herself then or after our session was occupying too much of my mental energy to be very effective. I told her—I don't recall the exact words—but something like it's too preoccupying for me to help you well. There was a look of surprise at this non-powerful and one-down position and at the self-disclosure it involved—whether she lived or died, and whether I could deliver effective therapy, mattered to me; it was not just a recitation of empathic clichés. She asked if I was really scared and I said I was. Her face and body softened.

It was not at this session—miracles don't happen in one 50-minute period—but it was at a relatively close in time session that Roberta asked me if I would take her scalpel and keep it safe somewhere, with a promise that I would give it back if she ever insisted. I knew she could get another such scalpel with minimal effort, but this one had symbolic value. It was *her scalpel, her insurance policy*. We wrapped the scalpel and the set of blades in a tissue, put it in a plastic bag, and put that in the bottom of a desk drawer. And there it stayed for years until her therapy was finished. She never asked for it back, and I eventually threw it out in an office move years later.

I don't know if I would do things the same way now. It can be risky to accept items such as knives, guns, or bags of saved-up medications ready for suicide, etc. But I suspect many trauma therapists have such stashes in their offices until they get the relationship on track enough for the client to agree to turn them over to a "discard unused medication" drive or to a police "reduce weapons risk" collection.

In reviewing how I might act now, after many more years of practice, I remain sure I would admit to the fear. I expect the principle with the dismissive client is, to find a way to show your caring is real, which eventually gets by the barriers. Getting by the barriers has often required taking a one-down position, rather than fighting the dismissive front. There's a fine line between acting helpless, which frightens the dismissive client, and acknowledging how the front makes it difficult to help them. It has worked to try to establish an agreed-upon metaphor for the behavior. One of the more useful ones was with a chronic help-rejecting complainer, where we used the metaphor of her "tying the therapist's hands" by her "yes but" behaviors.

It has also sometimes worked to gently remark that one feels "kept out." The trick is to emphasize the desire to really know the person, rather than expressing the therapist's frustration.

One other technique that sometimes works is to interpret what may be projective identification: "I wonder if you are unconsciously showing me how trapped and unable to do anything effective you felt in your family, by what is going on between us?"

All these have worked, sometimes . . .

The Disorganized/Chaotic Client

What of the chaotic client? The kind where *everything* is an emergency? With Frank and some others, the "solution" has been the centeredness of the therapist. Once, being interviewed for a job as clinical director at a Maine medical center that had a chaotic and disorganized psychiatric unit, the interviewer described what was needed for the job. He said, "What we need here is an old Maine flat-bottomed boat." Looking at the lobster boats out the window, I remembered how they went out in all kinds of weather and rode the crest of the waves without getting either swamped from the sides or horribly rocking and splashing and plunging and taking on water front to back.

Handling the chaotic client's emergencies requires the emotional attitude of that boat. The inner sense is consciously working at not being rocked: "It's all in the normal course of business; we do this every day, ho hum." Sort of the way surgeons casually talk about cutting open a patient and replacing some body part.

But that's important for the surgeon, and for the therapist. You want to communicate to the patient that you've seen this before and it's not an emergency to you.

Some of this was done in Frank's case simply by boundary management. When he would call with a crisis—many weekends had led to drunken, storm-out fights—the response was essentially, "Yes, I know it's upsetting; we'll talk about it more in your regular hour." The attitude was one of "refusing to engage in the perception that everything was a crisis and demanded an emergency response." "Yes, you and your wife often have blowouts; I'm sorry you went off the wagon last weekend. Maybe she will leave you for good this time, or not. She's stuck by you before. Let's talk more about it when you come in."

In ways, the client's chaos is just what they do, how they live. But in other ways, it's asking for a relational statement from the therapist.

I once had a shared administrative assistant who had a sign on her desk that captured the attitude: "The lack of planning on your part does not justify an emergency on mine." Or, less sarcastically, "I'm solid enough in this relationship not to need to join you in your panicked emotional state." The Tao says it as "hold fast to the center"(Tsu & Gia-Fu, 1989).

The statements of this attitude are sometimes:

"I hear you're upset and we can work it out when we talk at our regular time."

"I know this feels urgent, but you've gotten through these many times before."

"Well, if the relationship's in crisis, how might a couple's session sound" (if you do this kind of thing)?

The major focus is containing the chaos, bringing it into session, conveying you've "seen it before"; it may feel like a ten to them but for you it's a three; ho hum, let's just do the work. Then the internal chaos can come into the room and be worked on, rather than acted out all over the person's life and community.

10
THE EMPTY DEPRESSION

When I teach about the empty depression phase at workshops, I show a picture here of a hugely muscled wrestler-type man who has burst into tears. No matter what a person looks like on the outside, this is what it feels like on the inside to have been a victim of chronic and complex abuse. No matter the armor, the physique, the style, or social class, no matter all the surface defensive presentations, if a person is abused as a child, not loved enough, not protected, not provided secure attachment, it makes them sad. And scared. The core experiences of not being securely attached are fear, sadness, and shame, sometimes to the point of splitting an identity that has already been forming, or of preventing the coalescing of an identity in formation. Underneath it all, boiling it down to the core, chronic-trauma clients are full of grief and pain—and rage, which is the subject of the next chapter.

Persons who grow up without secure attachments feel empty, lonely, needy, and desperate inside. The emptiness fuels every kind of addiction, from food to drugs, to sex, to gambling, to spending. The self-blame fuels the addictive aspects of self-mutilation; it lets the pain out and/ or breaks the numbing. As a recent client said to me, "It's easier to feel the physical pain than the emotional." Too much emotional pain can lead to "decompensation," a word that doesn't really correspond to the experience. *The experience* is of terrifying shattering, falling into the void, screaming, being pulled apart, exploding. Kierkegaard called it "fear and trembling (Kierkegaard, 1985)."

The basic clinical task here is helping the client express the right amount of the emotion, the tolerable amount at the present time, while moving through the grief and out the other side, not wallowing in it (R. P. Kluft, 1984, 1993a, 1993c; R. P. Kluft, Kinsler, & O'Neil, 2014; Shapiro, 2001).

This is a demanding time for the therapist. Although it was likely complex, difficult, and troubling to get through those early defensive postures and attachment strategies of the client, this second phase demands the ability to sit with terrible sorrow over and over. For, in the years I have been doing it, the sorrow has been like a pot of soup that hasn't been stirred for a long time. It gets thicker and thicker the farther down you go. You and the client process grief and work on getting past it, moving through it. For a while the path down the river seems to lighten up but there are multiple storms ahead, each one deeper than the last. The therapist must be comfortable with holding deepest pain and sorrow, without defensively moving the client away from it. If you sit with yourself while a patient is experiencing this, you may well note your pulls to help them change the subject, or to offer empty rote reassurances, or to get pulled down into the pit of despair yourself, their hopelessness catching your deepest wounds.

Sometimes the hardest therapeutic task is just to sit there and "be with," without pulling back or distracting.

The basic relational lesson of the "being with" is that the patient is worth listening to. People are used to others trying to talk them out of their pain. They are met with "Yeah, buts" many times. "Yeah, but you had Grandma." "Yeah, but Uncle Larry took you fishing." "Yeah but the teachers loved how hard you worked to escape your home life." All these are probably true, but they are uttered for our comfort, because we do not want to touch the abyss.

Chronic childhood abuse has lifetime costs and leaves holes where connections should have lived. No one can become the mother you did not have at age 3. However much connection there is between therapist and client, we are not the mother they should have had. We cannot recompense the empty nights when someone should have been there to soothe the nightmares, or to prevent the abuser from having access.

We cannot be the admirer of the child's potential who should have been cheering them on as they learned to crawl, walk, ride a bike, throw a ball, or dance. There are Swiss cheese holes where there should have been filling experiences. Therapy cannot make up for what didn't happen at critical times in development of an emotional attachment system. We use fancy words like "allostatic load" to express the idea that a whole boatload of trauma is worse than half a load. We as therapists cannot go back and attend that first out-of-tune third grade band concert, and still cheer on our trombone-playing kid who tooted their best. We can identify these wounds and bind them, hoping that scabs form and they heal, and scar over. We can even aid the brain in recovering some capacities as our work helps restore damage to the limbic system (Chalavi et al., 2015). We cannot give a patient a childhood they never had.

What we can do is to "work through" the traumas until they no longer exert "as if it were still happening today" power. A client taught me about the power of touching the grief, shame, and profound self-hatred, of getting towards the bottom of that soup pot. As we talked about her being sold into prostitution by her family, she would put her face in her hands and cry, over and over, "Wanna disappear, wanna disappear, wanna disappear." She felt so despicable that the idea of death was preferable to how her experiences made her feel.

Whether done by a formal working-through of bad memories method such as EMDR, or a more interpersonally relational method, what we are striving to do is aid the client to come to a different idea of him or herself. From "wanna die" to "so sad" to "no child should have been put into that position" to "I as a child never deserved to be put into that position."

How do we get there?

No Evil Babies

It has proved useful to ask clients to observe babies and young children. I was lucky to have a college day care center with an outdoor playground accessible to my office. I might walk over with a client, or ask them to stop by. And then ask them whether they saw any evil babies or bad children there deserving of abuse. I've often used the line "I never met an evil baby." In many clients, this has led to a grudging openness to the idea that likely this client, as a baby, was not evil or deserving of abuse either. This creates a crack in the self-hatred and blame that is so debilitating to clients. The suggestion to have compassion for the baby they used to be is a powerful intervention. It has been hard for clients to maintain that they were the only baby born in human existence that deserved the abusive treatment received.

We are working towards "I didn't deserve that either." Every time we go deeper into that soup pot, hear the feelings, allow the expression of the pain and loss, *and then make an explicit connection for the client that no child deserved that treatment, we help the client move towards "working through."*

What does working through feel like to the client? It feels like the traumatic events are no longer happening now; they are "just a memory." They are no longer living in the hippocampus and other parts of the limbic system of their brain; instead, they have been operated on by the cortex. They have been "contextualized," if you will: That was then, this is now; it's no longer happening to me *and as a child I did not deserve that treatment. I was worth the same love and respect as any other baby/little kid.* We are moving through the grief and out the other side.

Nature Metaphors

One of the reasons we go to places of awe-inspiring natural beauty is to put the size of our own problems in perspective. Standing at the rim of the Grand Canyon, it's clear that I am a tiny speck in the universe, and as the famous philosopher Jackson Browne said, "In the end it's the wink of an eye."

Maybe because we all evolved from water, scenes involving the sea, flowing rivers, calm ponds, and waterfalls are often scenes that aid clients in putting their abuse histories into a less overwhelming perspective.

Lucky enough to live by a river, I often use river images in the work. The working through process can look like multiple foggy or stormy patches to move through as one goes down the river. And the effect of working through the trauma and coming out the other side can look like a clearer river and meadow.

A couple of caveats apply; we must always match our metaphors to the experiences of the client. If someone has reported experiences of water being used in their abuse experiences, obviously we do not use a water metaphor. We can seek from the client their imagined vision of a peaceful spot or a spot where they can heal, and use that spot as the end of the working-through journey for this part of abuse work. I no longer use the idea of a "safe place" for working through grief as so many clients have had no such thing. We design a healing place and a healing path.

Nature can put us all in our rather small place in the vastness, and in doing so diminish the enormity of what we feel. It can help make certain experiences "not such a big deal in the grand scheme of things."

The Use of Family History

Certainly, some people may be evil and terrible parents on a continuous basis. But this does not seem to be the majority. I have worked in many cases of termination of parental rights. Although sometimes extensive efforts to improve parenting result in repeated failures and relapses into whatever the parent's own symptomatic issues are—drugs, alcohol, addictions to frightful and abusive partners—often, these parents make massive efforts to improve their family and their parenting functioning. Many of these parents are terribly poor. In my experience, the wealthy don't often get pulled into the termination-of-rights process. Parents, with no reliable transportation, struggle to get the dead car running to make the supervised visit. They take food out of their own mouths to bring snacks to the visit at the parenting center. They are flawed, but when you make a parenting observation they are trying to cuddle their child, play with him or her, have fun, show bonding, show limit setting. Most failed parenting is actually ambivalent parenting—people trying hard and failing, or people trying hard to preserve their own very tenuous attachments while closing their eyes to the effects of their attachment to perpetrators on their own children.

This is not to excuse parents who expose children to abuse, neglect, substance abuse, or sexual harm. It is to say that in many of our cases, the abuse is not the whole story. We see the results of ambivalent and inadequate parenting most of the time, rather than just wholly "evil" parenting.

Why does this matter? They abused the child or exposed her/him to abuse, right? Here's where it matters: At the core, persons who have been severely abused conclude that this is what they were worth, as has been stated previously. However, often as clients begin to recover some sense of pride within the therapy, they might begin to "discover" evidence that abuse was not the whole story. Clients bring in family albums, pictures of their First Communion or first day of school, the birthday cards they are surprised to find their mother or father saved, the locks of hair, the baby pictures, the bronzed booties. This development is extremely useful in turning around the "nobody loved me" internal narrative. The narrative can change to "my screwed-up mother did love me, she was just too _____ whatever, fill in the blank, to bring me up well." "My lousy father held on to this picture of my First Communion in his wallet till the day he went into the nursing home," etc. Although sometimes this may be an indication of the parent being in denial of the harm he/she caused, it is more often in my experience an expression of their love and wish to do well, even if they failed.

In observing this, it has proved helpful to facilitate it. As the patient's self-respect begins to grow, the therapist can ask them if they have family mementoes, or memories of good times, vacations that were not terrible, or good alone times with one or the other parent. The recognition of some good experiences within the family can begin to pry the putty out of the bricks of the wall and begin to let some light shine through. Be alert for them; sense when they can be heard and felt; ask for them.

The Death or Disability of Perpetrators

Maintaining loyal connections to perpetrators is often one of the major functions of critical superegos in better-organized patients, or of the role of persecutor personalities in dissociative patients. Clients adopt to Dad's expectations and make them part of their own psyche, as one sign of loyalty, fealty to family, and mammalian submission. Clients create a persecutor part to avoid pain and maintain what love there is by enforcing the unhealthy system's rules. Clients take in the family taboos to stay safe and possibly "make themselves lovable." The therapist whose care is essentially non-conditional—or at least has far wider and healthier boundaries than those of the family of origin—is attempting to get taken in, introjected, as a counterweight to the persecutor messages.

One of the most powerful times of change I have seen comes about with the death or disability of the primary perpetrator.

In Laurie, our ambivalent/preoccupied client's case, her abusing father died of natural causes well into his eighties. She became suicidal and chaotically switched, not functioning at home, leaving "child parts"—her child-like dissociative states—in charge when she needed to take care of her biological children. She was hospitalized on our local psych unit, and I was called in. As I entered the room, this normal-sized woman in her fifties suddenly boomed out in an angry male voice that sounded like it came from a 250-pound linebacker, "*I work for YOU now???*" I wish I could say that I had a wonderfully snappy and savvy answer to that. I suspect it was more something like, "Well, uhhhh, ummm, ahhh, not exactly." I was able, however, eventually, to use this incident as an opportunity to help turn around this "persecutor part" of Laurie's dissociative mind into the actual role in her internal system of personalities, that is, as a protector from further harm. The strategy was to tell this part of the mind (manifested by the angry male voice) that his power and strength had been previously needed and his prior efforts to keep "the body" out of trouble with "the father, were appreciated" but that in therapy he could learn how to be more effective in the new circumstances. Rather than punishing the other parts of Laurie's mind for thinking of violating her father's rules or acknowledging his harmfulness, I could teach this part how to be a more effective protector. Grudging acceptance on his part led eventually to alliance with the therapist and a request to change his name from "The Bad Man" to "Persecutor/Protector." Over time the persecutor feelings and behaviors dropped off and the former internal torturer/protector became the best treatment ally.

A similar pattern emerged in Roberta, the armored/dismissive client we have followed. In this case, the primary perpetrator was killed in a home invasion. Roberta was sufficiently rocked when this happened that I made a home visit, something I rarely did. I was aware that our therapy had become the container for more than that surgical scalpel. The ability to be safe and protected had been projected on to me in something of a magical thinking way—somehow the connection between us was going to keep her from being hurt again. This was not the time to process this non-reality–based way of relating to me. That could be done when things were less in crisis. The relational task here became to provide a rock to lean on while the police and fire departments and the medical examiners did their jobs. And then to respectfully withdraw when the client's other support systems began to show up and her defenses became more engaged. Going through this with her, saying very little, but sitting at her kitchen table holding her hand as the authorities did their initial work "got in." I was not merely an office presence. I was *there* when it mattered, and, afterwards, I was much more *there* as an introjected object in her psyche.

Roberta had a dissociative disorder that operated in its own unique way, as many such clients do. She once described her internal world as a bunch of mountaintops shrouded by fog (many clients have rich metaphors to describe themselves) and often when she felt that she had switched to a different "mountain," that way of functioning could be in front and in charge for a long period. In other words, she had encapsulated major ways of relating to the outside world and these were complex and well organized, but felt separate from each other, and when one part came to the front, other ways of operating were unavailable for lengthy periods.

Being present during this crisis yielded the feeling of becoming part of her mountain range, becoming a part that could help clear off the fog and contribute towards the cooperation or coalescence of the others.

The relational messages, sent intentionally, were:

1. You are important enough in this crisis for me not to worry about traditional boundaries in your time of greatest pain.
    a. I know we have worked together long enough that this break in the structure will not lead you to terror.

b. I know we have worked together long enough that this break in the structure will not lead you to make unnecessary demands when it is not this acute.

c. I am a real person and I care about you.

d. I will get out of the way when it's time.

e. I don't expect any special thanks for being human at this moment.

f. This is a time to put up or shut up, and I'm putting up.

g. To say, "Oh, this must be hard; let's talk next Wednesday at our 11 o'clock" would be disrespectful.

h. That I recognize just how difficult it is for you to let down the dismissive defenses.

i. That the real relationship between us means I support you when a major crisis occurs. It is important enough for me to stretch myself.

j. It's probably this real relationship that is most curative anyway.

There were no negative repercussions from this home visit; there was appreciation and a deepening of real connection and an advance of healing. It felt like our relationship now stood on bedrock, and that I had become a dependable figure in this client's inner world.

I'm certain that many colleagues would never think of stepping out of their offices, or at most would only go so far as meeting someone at an emergency department. At the start of my career, I had two experiences that made this action possible. The first was as a caseworker for the New York City Department of Social Services, making home visits, and finding out how valuable it was to see people in their real situations. The second was some six years being part of or running psychiatric emergency services, which often involved meeting or accompanying the police to the house of a highly suicidal or mentally ill person. Some of these people might later become clients. I never found being in their home harmful; it always led to having a deeper sense of the truth of their lives.

The point is we make intervention choices that are workable for us and that we believe will further undergird the work, and that with this population we must constantly monitor these choices and discuss their meanings with the client. Exceptions can be made when a situation is urgent. There is a difference between violating boundaries vs. stretching them when it is central to relational healing.

The deaths of Laurie and Roberta's perpetrators were actual deaths, but one can use an imagined death as a technique. This is combined with future prediction. "Imagine that X has died. Let the fact of his/her death penetrate. How do you feel? What, if anything, has let go? Can you hold that feeling inside as we come back to the present?"

Grief Work in Dreams

What of our chaotic client? How did Frank do his grief work? I wish there were an explicit story to tell about how that work got done, but most of it seems to have been internal, as both his wife and I were regularly there for him, did not punish or scorn, but did not follow him around in every drama and/or rescue him. The client eventually told us this was working in a dream:

The client came in to a regularly scheduled appointment and said, "Doc, I had the weirdest dream!" I don't do much dream interpretation, but this opening obviously required a respectful follow-up question. I asked him to tell me more about it.

"I was walking down the hall in a hospital. I didn't recognize it; it was one of those old-fashioned ones. I realized I was in the maternity ward. They had all the babies in cradles behind one of those big windows. I looked at them all and then tried to walk down the hall. But one of those babies was calling to me. I knew what was going to happen to that baby! I looked at the baby and I said, "No one is going to love you, baby. No one wants you, baby. People are going to do terrible things to you, baby. You're gonna get beat, and starved, and locked in a closet, baby. And they're going to make you do sex things that really hurt! No one loves you, baby. No one wants you, baby."

"And so, I turned away from the window and tried to walk down the hall but that baby kept calling me back. Every time it did, I told it how it was going to be abused for years and years, and in all kinds of ways.

But the baby kept calling me back and calling me back. Finally, I went into the nursery and I walked over to the bassinet and I picked up the baby and I said, "No one's going to love you, baby. No one's going to take care of you, baby. You're gonna get beat and raped and locked in closets, baby. No one's going to care about you, baby . . . so, I guess, I'm going to have to adopt you, baby."

And then this very chaotic blue-collar man lifts his head out of his reverie and brings himself back to the present; he looks at me in the eye and says, "So now, doc, everything I do I got this baby under my arm and I gotta ask, 'Is this good for the baby???'" We both laughed. He had taken in his need to nurture his own damaged and fragile self.

Notes on Dissociative Patients

The working through of grief is more complex for the dissociative patient, as are most of the phases of treatment discussed previously. Here are some of the extra challenges of this phase experienced with dissociative patients:

1. Alter states have different feelings about their childhood experiences. There are likely to be bereft alters, "undamaged" ones protected by the others, amnestic ones, punishing ones. Each one will likely need to process the experience through their own perceptual lenses, though it is often possible to shorten this process by creating internal teams, groups, or alliances to face certain emotional tones of the work.
2. There need to be systematic internal communication and cooperation tools available to the client's system to allow processing through the different alternate personalities. If internal communication has not already been established, working with the grief of one state of mind can result in punishment/self-mutilation by another and denial by a third.
    a. Permissive hypnosis is an invaluable tool here.
        i. "Your whole mind will know just which parts of yourself can be here for this piece of work."

ii. "Please have the group we have put together to do this work step forward. The others can close their eyes or go to sleep if that is the right thing to do."

iii. "Ask all those who can tolerate this work to hold hands and come together and out front to discuss this."

iv. "Your unconscious mind will know just the right arrangement to make so the right parts of you can feel this."

v. "Remember how Susie said she would hold the baby while we talk about this? Your whole mind will know how and where Susie and the baby should be while we do this work."

vi. "Let's go to the healing place we designed, and your whole self will know what arrangement to make there so no one is too scared or broken while we do this work."

3. A sense of pace is required. Too much, too deep, too many alternate personalities exposed to the trauma and its impact can re-traumatize the patient. How much can they tolerate, when? Are there middle-level abuse experiences to grieve about that can then generalize to both more and less intense ones? Principles of learning continue to operate even in the dissociative mind.

4. It is dangerous to attempt the grief work without the major persecutor states of mind on board. Their reaction is likely to be internal (i.e., shame attacks, blaming) and external punishment for talking, betraying family secrets, breaking the bond with the perpetrator, etc. The redefinition of the perpetrator as a protector, as the one who saved the child from even worse, should be an antecedent to this step. In general, most persecutor alters have some loyalty to the smallest, baby states, and this can often be used to "turn" the persecutor towards recognizing their protective role:

a. Therapist: "You came about when 'the bad man' told her she'd better not talk, right?"

Persecutor/Alternate Personality/State of Mind: "Damn right. If that stupid kid talked he'd really give it to us. She should just shut up and take her medicine."

Therapist: "So weren't you just trying to prevent her from being hurt worse?"

Persecutor: "Damn right, that dope could a got us all killed. She's a whimpering imbecile."

Therapist: "So she needed your protection to keep her from screwing it all up?"

Persecutor: "If it wasn't for me we'd be dead and he'd have killed the little sister too."

Therapist: "Thank you for keeping them safe. I know you 'punished' them to keep it from getting even less safe; you were protecting them."

Persecutor: "Well, I guess."

Therapist: "You know, you as a whole person needs that strength now. I can help you find a better way to use it."

5. It is important to watch for internal shifts, small integrations (comings together of alternate personalities), alternate personalities "fading" as this work goes on. Sometimes, when one alter processes an experience, it generalizes to others and the reason for being separate disappears. Amnesia between alters is a felt experience for the client rather than an objective, external reality. Lab experiments show transfer of information where alters believe they have no memories (Dorahy et al., 2014). Working through grief for one "part of the mind" sometimes obviates the need for the felt presence of "another part of the mind." You get mini-integrations.

Summary

It is often best to do the grief work before the anger work, if possible. Clients do not always give us that option. Moving the grief towards "Hey, I really didn't deserve that" is an energizing step, one that can catalyze anger expression and provide energy and force to the person's continued development and healing.

11
OMNIVOROUS RAGE

If someone hurts us, we get angry. It's so important to our survival that it's one of the built-in emotions (Nathanson, 1997a, 1997b). It's the fight part of fight, flight, freeze, or faint. Little kids usually cannot fight back very well without provoking further abuse and/or abandonment. Yet, many do it all the time, often quite indirectly, acting out, behaving as if they have a true ADHD, sneaking around, or more productively, through sports or other achievements that anger may fuel. However, when dependent on an abuser, anger can equal danger if expressed directly. So, it gets stored in the limbic system of the brain and in the muscles. It's no wonder trauma survivors have so many musculoskeletal and immune system issues. All that physical tension of wanting to strike out must go somewhere and often gets somaticized.

In our case, anger is a useful fuel. When we are successful in doing grief work, anger can emerge. Or, if the client is perpetually angry, we can know that there is deep grief to be excavated. If possible, we try to direct the anger towards making major differences in self-statements, in our beliefs and thoughts about ourselves:

"I'm unlovable → Those bastards didn't love me right → I did deserve to be loved right → I'll treat myself as worthy of love → I'll accomplish things in my life to show them → I'll accomplish things in my life because I'm worth it." The sequence is from deep shame to self-respect.

Client Fears

When clients withhold anger expression for years, they often believe that if they start feeling it, it will never end. Anger is perceived as an omnivorous monster that will consume everything: the client, the therapist, the room, the clinic, the building, the world. There is tremendous fear of feeling it, lest it destroy everything and especially, everyone.

Clients fear rejection, especially by the therapist, as so many others have rejected them. Clients also fear that if they express the anger, they may physically harm the therapist. Clients fear that their fragile sense of wholeness will shatter if they touch the anger. Clients fear that the anger will fill the room, the entire hour, the leave-taking, and then the "world." The fear of shattering of self, or other, is palpable.

Certainly, premature expression of stored anger can destabilize both the patient and their life situation. And, if not done in a contained and predictable and managed manner, it could destroy the therapy relationship and other relationships. Therefore, it is best if possible to do the anger work after the grief work. There's less stored energy behind it.

However, in truth, in a well-bounded therapy relationship, clients tend to express anger for moderate periods of time, generally within 15 to 20 minutes in my experience. It turns out not to be the all-consuming and all destroying monster that people fear.

I should add that this is *not true* if the client is encouraged to "just express their feelings" from the beginning of therapy. In such cases, there is neither the relational holding environment, the safety of the structure of the therapy, the experience of emotions being manageable, and the building of skills to manage them that exists in a therapy that's been reasonably well managed through the stages discussed here. Want to blow up a treatment? Just start asking clients to express their feelings without any training in how to do that safely. We are not talking about catharsis here, about "blowing it out." We are talking about manageable moderate-level anger expression that does not destabilize.

Notes on Dissociative Clients

As we have been saying all along, dissociation and a diagnosis of dissociative identity disorder (DID) vastly complicates the work. In many dissociative patients, there are separate-feeling parts of the mind whose internal job is to hold anger and perhaps nothing else. These parts do and can feel angry enough to blow up the delicate balances and arrangements among the alternate personalities inside the patient. They often have frightening names—"the monster," "the demon from the gates of hell," "the destroyer." The other parts of the mind often live in fear of this part. In child-like trance logic, it feels like that part of the mind can kill everyone and everything, inside and outside, and be all-consuming.

This is where the building of internal alliances is so crucial along with the use of counter-trance. Let's take Frank's case, the chaotic one. After the dream in which he adopted his abandoned and abused baby-self, he now had to ask if every action he took was good for the baby. This is the kind of alliance that can be used to facilitate moderate and tolerable anger expression: "Can you tell me how angry you felt about X in a way that's not going to destabilize the baby?" "Can you express the rage in a way that doesn't frighten the kids you are trying to protect?" "What part of the mind inside can help you talk about and feel this without everything inside you blowing up?" "What's a mid-level experience that made you angry but isn't so big it shatters everyone?" And, as usual, permissive hypnosis: "Your mind and self will know the right internal arrangement and the right events to let out some of the anger without coming apart."

If you have established a supposed physical "location" for the organization of the mind, use it. "Remember the house inside where you said all the parts live? Ask just the right parts to come to the family meeting room. You'll know who should come and who should listen outside the door and who should stay in their own room." The drawing together of the "right parts" to express some anger, while taking into consideration the safety of the whole person/other parts, can aid in establishing internal cooperation and coherence—the person is thinking of him or herself as a whole, existing within one location/body, all of whose needs must be considered. Always working towards enhancing internal cooperation, alliances, and communication, with the strong implication that the other parts "will soon be ready." Also, that eventually the other parts who, after all, live in the same "body/house," will come to the family meeting room "when they are ready."

Therapist Fears

Therapists have their own struggles with hearing and managing anger. No one likes to be screamed at. No one likes to fear physical harm. On a more superficial but still significant level, no one wants to walk out of their office and have colleagues say, "Boy, what the heck was going on in there? That screaming frightened me and my patient!" And we have our own particular placement on the Wilson and Lindy empathy matrix (Wilson & Lindy, 1994). Those of us drawn to too much attunement can have our own anger hooked by the patient's. How many times have you come out of a session feeling that you'd like to give that parent a piece of your mind, or even belt them? I certainly have. These therapist feelings can be good and useful or they can fog the choices we make. We can recruit too much anger too fast, or encourage actions dangerous to our clients. For a time, it was something of a fad to encourage clients to confront their abusers, sue their abusers, etc. This often backfired, especially when a client was not healed or stable enough to experience what usually happens: a perpetrator's denial, reciprocal rage at them, denying of their reality, continued betrayal by non-offending others, etc. They might have difficulty tolerating the emotional stress of a multi-year court process with an uncertain and likely unsatisfying outcome. Or a decade of attack by false-memory advocates.

If any "confrontation" of perpetrators is contemplated, it often requires months of preparatory work. The client should be walked through all the foregoing scenarios. What's going to happen when your father says you're crazy? What's going to happen when your mother says, "He was a good man and would never do such things . . . and you are an ungrateful, mentally ill, unlovable brat."

The only time I have seen these confrontations work was when the client had a stack of prepared index cards on which she had written every likely defensive or attacking phrase or strategy of her abuser, and worked with the therapist on how she would respond verbally, and in her feelings and concepts of self.

Therapists on the less attuned end of the spectrum can and do turn off as the client gets angry, sending out messages that the client is "too emotional," "childish," "just a labile borderline." "Not manageable in individual therapy." Such therapists confirm the client's worst fears: If they get angry, they will lose the therapist. Therapists of this makeup likely need supervision/peer consultation to determine how to be less rigid and judgmental with the inevitable anger expressed by the chronically abused client, and to avoid distancing and one-up, demeaning statements such as "just use your skills."

I once consulted on a case in which a therapist spent a year avoiding doing trauma work with a client because "her skills were not in place." The client was on an internal boil, the pressure cooker's relief valve was blowing steam, and all the therapist could do was murmur empty phrases about skill-building. This was a perversion of the initial safety and stability phase of treatment, in which the client's experience was ignored until they had "done their homework." The phases of treatment are guidelines and are not rigid rules and do not replace thoughtful clinical judgment. In this case, safety and stability would have been enhanced by working towards allowing moderate-level anger expression.

How do you tell the difference? How do you know when to stick to the script and when to ad lib? This requires attempting to codify and teach clinical judgment. Hard to do. Here are some thoughts: The first "law of holes" is if you're in a hole, stop digging. If technique A isn't working, rather than sticking rigidly to the model, try technique B. Monitor the trajectory of the therapy. If there's no change and growth, no upward slope, modify what you're doing. Therapists tend to stick to their preferred approach. Although a focus on client strengths and resilience is important, therapist statements such as "Oh, I only like to focus on strengths" is likely useless if one is dealing with a genocide survivor. It's denying the client's core experiences. Try to compile within your mind or notes the major themes of the client's life and self-system. Which of these is the most cause of trouble? How can you design a therapy relationship that is a counter to these core beliefs? "Nice" isn't good enough, nor is "firm boundaries." The "nice" needs to be directed towards the wounds, to counteract the deep self-system learnings. In the stuck case discussed previously, a little bit of "I can see where you'd be angry and hurt" would have gone a long way past "keep practicing your breathing." The central idea is to be sensitive to the client's meta-message and perform a therapy that is a counter meta-message. So, "I'm angry all the time" can be heard and then used. "I hear how bad this hurt you, how mad this made you, and you know I don't see you the way your parents did. And you're angry because somewhere deep down you know the way you were treated wasn't right. How can we use that knowing to move your life forward? Somewhere there's a spark of pride or else you wouldn't be angry. If that spark of pride could talk, what would it say to your parents? Your husband? What does it want to do with your life?" *Turn the anger to pride and motivation.*

The "firm boundaries" also needs to be used in a counter meta-message way. "Notice that when you get angry here, I listen to you, don't retaliate, but try to make sure you're contained enough to leave safely? That's a way of saying I care enough to try to de-escalate so you don't come out feeling out of control. I remember how many completely out-of-control screaming matches you told me your parents had. I don't want you to have to experience that here. We can let anger out and move on." Whether said explicitly or only acted implicitly, the boundaries are again a counter meta-message, from the message that the client's emotions, and those of the world in response, are not containable, vast, destructive, shattering to "Eh, so you get angry some, so what, not going to blow *us* apart."

If we think about a standard seven-point Lykkert scale with 0 as the midpoint and ± 3 points on either side, as I reflect, I think I am regularly trying to help the client balance between hurt and anger from +2 to −2, not too far in either direction. It's a felt sense but with conscious attention to the knowledge that staying on either end of the spectrum is almost never health giving.

The Magic Remote Control

The *magic remote control* is a hypnotic technique that is immensely useful in processing grief and anger. It uses the fact that many chronic-abuse survivors use self-hypnosis and/or dissociation to cope with the original trauma and are good at it. Trauma therapists should pursue formal training in hypnosis, and nothing in these chapters substitutes for that training; however, it is helpful to talk about the usefulness of various techniques.

The core of this one is the idea that we can imaginatively manipulate reality to make experiences more tolerable. So, "Imagine a TV remote. And a TV screen. There's a button to make the screen bigger or smaller, and one for nearer or farther away. There's a slider for how intense the feelings are when viewing the screen. There's a button for start and stop. There's a slider for compression of time. . ." "We can move through this experience as fast or slow as your mind thinks is right." "There's a slider for how old you feel while watching this." "Your unconscious mind will know if there are any other controls that will help you with this experience."

"Let's have you look at a neutral experience on the screen. Make it bigger. Make it smaller. Move it closer. Move it farther away. Use the slider to decide how fast it should go. Let's go through that neutral experience at a count of ten. How was that?"

"Now, we're going to use it for that moderate-level experience that made you angry that we discussed last time. Put the screen at the right size and distance and look at it while using parts of your mind that are the right age to cope with it. Now, move through the experience, controlling how fast you move and how intense your feelings are. You can push stop at any time, or change how fast or slow you move. OK, let yourself look at the screen and let's go through that experience and out the other side." I first learned this technique from Richard Kluft and have seen it expanded upon since by many others (R. P. Kluft, 1993a, 1993d).

Titrated Anger

What we're looking for here is titrated anger expression—enough to unlock the limbic system–cortex connection without triggering freeze or faint. We know that experiences generalize. By picking a moderate-level traumatizing event and working it through, the person experiences a reduction in all the events triggering significant anger. It is not necessary to process every anger-making event. Processing a moderate-level event typically reduces the overall burden. And, the person can then review his/her life and decide if there are other events that need to be processed. The client has the experience of successfully processing anger, not getting destabilized, being able to think about the event rather than just being overwhelmed by the feelings, and developing a personal sense of power and control.

Not Getting Stuck in It

It's crucial to aid the client in not getting stuck in the trauma and frozen in time. Moving forward through the experience should be emphasized. Letting time flow. Moving through it. Out the other side. Should the client begin to get stuck, the fallback position is the other various containment and control strategies:

"Ok, that one's still scary. So, let's move the TV farther back and make the screen smaller. Let's push the stop button. Let's eject the DVD. Let's take that DVD and put it in a lead-lined box. Let's put that box at the bottom of a mine shaft and fill that shaft in," etc. The message is: "We have control of this re-experiencing and can start or stop it and prevent it from taking over your experience." This is a powerful message for persons whose lives have often been totally out of their control. I owe a great debt here to Richard Kluft, who helped to develop and has taught these techniques for years (R. P. Kluft, 1985, 1993a, 2006, 2012a).

Use the Energy

Anger is forceful and energetic. In this model of therapy, it is used to propel the client from a stuck space to the next developmental task. This task is breaking the social isolation that so frequently is the lot of the chronic-trauma survivor. In so many cases, the therapy becomes the person's life. There is nothing more important than that hour or two hours a week. Every facet of life is focused on the therapy. Often there are no other relationships, or very few. The client travels hundreds of miles to see the "trauma specialist." Or through snow squalls, dust storms, unremitting heat. Therapy can be a life saver and the focus of life.

And, after the anger is expressed and the hurt processed, a wider vision begins to emerge. The client, rather than staring down at the railroad tracks at their feet, begins to look up and see a road, a path, somewhere to go. Educational opportunities beckon. Careers open. There is a growth of quiet self-respect and self-esteem. Others begin to recognize these changes and are drawn to the person who used to live in isolation. Friendship and social engagements arise, and we are into the next phase, the reconnection to the world.

Let's look at this anger-launching pattern in the three patients we've been following.

For Frank, the need to care for his internal baby led to far less impulsive behavior. His business had previously been as chaotic as the rest of his life. He'd miss appointments, blow deadlines, have fights with customers, have fights with employees, blow afternoons deciding he had a right to go off and drink the day away because something had been frustrating.

What happened for him was increased steadiness. He made his business appointments, turned up when he said he was going to do so. His business, always teetering between grandiose ideas and failure to perform, began to become steady. He had taken on a contract to do repairs of lawnmowers, chain saws, and brush cutters for several large local institutions, including a school district and a college. Although his work was good, it often took him months to attend to a job. It was maddening to his clients when he was so unpredictable or when a machine would sit on his shelf for a year.

Now, he started to get along with some employees, where he had been impossible to work for before. His trucks and repair people were where they were supposed to be. His repair schedule was actually a schedule, and people could count on him. And different relationships began to form, to be discussed later.

Roberta, our hospital queen, stopped demanding Mr. Perfect and settled down with "Mr. guy who had loved her for many years but wasn't good enough for her." They had two children. She began to develop an interest in spirituality and made a career change, all of which are discussed in more detail in the next chapter.

And our ambivalent/preoccupied Laurie? After the main perpe-trator's death, there was significant work to do on the failure of her mother to protect her. But, after this was done, changes began to happen with her husband and her children, and to move much more into "just another therapy" mode, rather than the incredibly intense and draining work of years.

Let's look at this re-entry phase in more detail.

12

REBUILDING THE
DEVASTATED LIFE

Sitting Duck Phenomenon

Kluft and Freyd have taught us that when one learns to wear blinders around our abusive parents, to "not see" abuse, this perceptual style generalizes. The child learns to "not notice" that the basketball coach's head pats are moving to become more intimate. To "not see" that the proposed mate who needs to call on his/her cell phone 20 times a day is not "so in love" but "so needing control." To not see the repeated arrest history as representative of a moral or character defect, but to blame it on people picking on the poor guy/gal.

Let's say that a girl is abused regularly by her father at night after her mother is asleep. When she hears the footsteps coming down the hall, she knows what is going to happen. But her father is also the warmer parent, and the one everyone on the outside says is such a good guy. Boy Scout Leader. Church Elder. Beloved coach. As Jennifer Freyd has taught us, the child must learn not to see what was done to her, to unconsciously preserve the illusion of a safe family and a safe world (J. J. Freyd, 1996; J. J. Freyd & Birrell, 2013; R. P. Kluft, 1993a, 1993c, 1993d). So, the child becomes adept at *not perceiving and/or immediately dismissing danger signs*. *"Oh, that couldn't be; he seems so nice."*

Learning not to notice and/or to push away danger signals removes one of the life-sustaining functions of anxiety—signaling that something is not right: "Hmmm, it smells like a saber-tooth tiger around here; better get out." And so the patient becomes a sitting duck for users and abusers.

And one of the main tasks of this phase of therapy is reopening the eyes to both danger and the possibility of love and safety and comfort.

The Perception of Aloneness

Child abuse is generally isolating. In most cases, it is to be a secret from everybody else. And should the child be abused in groups, there are other pressures and threats to keep it a secret.

Abusers use every kind of threat and manipulation to silence the child:

"If you say anything, no one will believe you."

"I'll know if you say anything, and it will get worse."

"Children who tell get taken away from their mothers."

"Watch me nearly run over this pet, and understand what will happen if you talk."

"If the two of you rat me out, you'll get separated into two different foster homes and never see each other again."

"This gun I'm firing in the air now—what do you think will happen if you talk?"

And, of course, the highly insidious "I'm doing this because I love you and someone has to teach you." Or, "I'm doing this because we're so close, and this is what people close to each other do."

The secrecy and threats leave the child survivor blind to future threat and bereft of confidants, feeling utterly alone. Alone makes for believing "there's nobody out there." And alone makes for vastly empty and needy. Either side of that pole makes it hard to find friends or partners.

The Perception of Emptiness

To the client, the legacy of abuse can leave a black hole of needy feelings. As children, we have a right to expect our parents and connected community members and organizations to nurture and fill us. We get so-called narcissistic supplies from interactions with our parents, grandparents, extended family, school, church or synagogue or mosque, etc.

When we are not filled by those whose job it is to fill us, we are left figuratively screaming to be filled.

On a trip to Maine, we were lost and looking for the LL Bean main store. We had stayed at a motel before and knew we were close to the right route. We decided, in the days before GPS, navigation, and smartphones, to ask the desk clerk. She was a rather stern-looking Yankee lady resembling for all the world the woman in the famous Grant Wood portrait of a farmer and his wife, with the husband holding a pitchfork. She kind of cackled and then said, "Go out on the highway over there. Open your wallet and follow the large sucking sound!"

One of the saddest consequences of an extended abuse history is that the person seeking remediation of their emptiness often feels to others like that large sucking sound, and it pushes people away, making the survivor even more bereft.

In truth, no one can fill that emptiness, and trying to do so sets the person up for such struggles. Shel Silverstein once wrote a little book entitled "The Missing Piece," describing how this works in leading relationships to failure and how one must find their own missing piece (Silverstein, 1976).

Therapy cannot fill the client's emptiness, but it can and does contribute to the budding of a sense of worth. As the grief and rage are towards the natural ends of their processing, the client's felt sense of self changes. Remember from the anger chapter how there is naturally a shift in which the power of the anger deeply diminishes the sense of shame and it begins to be replaced with a sense of worth? This sense of worth, no matter how tentative, affects how the person presents him/herself in the world. We are biological animals, and we're hard-wired to read the power and threat potential of other humans. We notice body posture, shoulder hunching, the quality of the other's steps, their breathing, their eye contact. Somewhere in those instantaneous evaluations we know how much pride and how much doubt and how much need the other person is carrying. And as our, so to speak, "vibrations" change, the world reacts differently.

There Are No Resources for Me!

Often without specific interventions or directions, if as the old cliché goes, "God willing and the creek don't rise," clients' empty lives begin to shift, something the therapist is there to witness and applaud without having to do anything about it in particular. The client *reports* that the volunteer coordinator at the Red Cross appeared to take her/him more seriously. That he/she was asked to join a committee or the men's group at church. That suddenly he/she got included in the workplace invitation to go to the Red Sox/Yankees game.

Clients who used to be so closed within their own fortresses gradually lower the footbridge and drain the moat, and others react.

Life as a Succession of Attitudes

A brilliant client once taught me that "life is a succession of attitudes." Our attitudes aid in determining how others react to us. This can be sadly misused and overstated when and if people come to believe they can "manifest" any outcome by the attitude they put out towards the "universe." This is too far in the magical thinking direction. I've had a client who has been "manifesting" winning the lottery for 15 years now. Seems she is still working for a living.

However, in relationships with others we often get what we present ourselves as being worth.

A conventionally classically beautiful woman spent years saying there was just no one out there for her; no one in her rural community with her education; no one who appreciated art and music the way she did; no one raised essentially in her social class. A Brahmin from a now-impoverished Boston family, she was doomed to aloneness in the family's former summer house, a place she had withdrawn to when all the wealth disappeared. And in truth she was alone, crying, empty, and bereft feeling. Her one relationship with someone "far beneath her" had left her a single parent of a difficult adolescent, with no supportive social relationships. There was great bitterness within the family over the loss of finances and position; over who had screwed over whom; who had gotten the better share of what little was left; what they were going to do with the family silver in the wilds of northern Vermont, where there was little need for high tea. In truth, she had no dating relationships for years.

In the kind of family she was raised in, she was a "failure" for having a child with whom she did. She was shameful for not completing her education and serving in the Diplomatic Corps. She had never been "enough," and a history of sexual abuse had left her afraid of her own appearance and disowning her own sexuality.

The guy with the black hat in her movie was her father. His life was spent at very high levels of government and finance, moving easily from one to the other. He made bad investments just before a market crash and had the gall to have a heart attack and die just as things were falling apart. "Daddy" was an unassailable icon in her mind who would have rescued the whole situation had he lived. But Daddy always favored her brother and saw her as defective from the time she started dating "what's his name." There was deeply impacted grief work to do.

How was this work accomplished? With this patient, it took time/ years before idealized Daddy was ready to be left behind. The therapy relationship gathered gravitas when there was a crisis about her child and she could grieve and rage over his acting out, and how little her remaining family had done to help. This chink in the armor could then be used to open up that "the whole picture wasn't really that ideal, was it?" She began to drop the idea that all her problems were due to "chronic, refractory depression" and the hope that the next SSRI or "enhancing" medication would "make her better." Probing questions were asked such as: "What did it feel like not to live up to Daddy's wishes?" "How did it feel that he really didn't take care of anyone, but gambled the whole family's future?" "What was it like to see your brother always the apple of his eye, and for you never to be able to do anything right after you got pregnant in college?" This was a process of knowing where the wound lay and poking around for openings. Eventually we hit the gusher and tears flowed, anger arose and was expressed, followed by an increase in self-valuing and a rejection of Daddy's opinion and her mother's cutoff.

Sometime later she attended a community art show, previously beneath her. But as her grief work had been done, her need to hold onto "all the fixings" of her upbringing began to drop away and so she attended local events.

And she looked at and chatted with a man who she previously would not have noticed. Old sweater, white beard, body like Santa Claus. Last I knew they were still married.

Recognizing Openings

The hardest part of conveying this work to others is teaching when there is an opening into the client's core beliefs about self and world. There are no bright lights and green paths like in some financial investment commercials. Here are things worth being sensitive to, as you and the client are coming through processing the grief and anger:

1. The spark of "Yes, I was worth more than that" in speech or in the way the client carries him/herself.
    a. Be aware of changes in how folks talk about themselves and how their posture, gait, and eye contact change.
    b. Point these changes out and acknowledge them. "Did you notice how you're walking differently?" "Did you notice that last time your brother refused to help, you got enraged and also down on yourself for not being able to do it yourself? Now you only reacted about what a selfish ass he was and got help elsewhere! You didn't take his behavior in!"
2. Subtle cues that the client's behavior is changing without their noting the changes or how these are attached to their sense of self:
    a. The client stops disparaging going to Al Anon.
    b. They make a new social contact.
    c. They attend an event and are immediately drawn to the kind of person who is their poison but, after the momentary orienting response, rather than moving towards that eventually painful object, they are now disgusted.
3. Complaints about the spouse or partner drop out and are replaced by discussions of how family issues are now being negotiated much more collaboratively.

a.   One of the clients presented earlier in this book, our ambiva-
lent/preoccupied client, Laurie, began therapy years ago saying
she just wanted to have "normal person problems." After years
of work on the anger and grief of all the parts that needed to
do that work, one day we were talking about her son's application to prep school, her husband's contemplation of whether
to accept a promotion or change employers for better opportunities, and her daughter's play on the woman's hockey team,
when she suddenly looked up and made eye contact, chortled
and said, "Phil, we're talking about normal person problems!"
Shortly we began to move towards termination.

Wondering Towards Health

"I wonder if . . ." As noted previously, this question stem is useful in
many aspects of treatment in recruiting the client's observing ego and
getting that function within the client allied with the therapist. As used
in a rebuilding-your-life phase, it can avoid resistance. "I wonder if that
church group might have changed since you last tried it?" "I wonder
whether there's an AA group for professionals around?" "I wonder what
ever happened to that woman you met at the conference?"

The attitude of the therapist is crucial here. The mental picture is of a
parent comforting the child with the skinned knee but also sort of shoo-
ing them back outside to play again with the attitude "it's no big deal,"
"you can do it." Sort of waving one's hands in the "back outside and
try again direction." Any way you gently go about doing this will likely
work. The idea is slowly encouraging the patient to take interpersonal
risks just beyond their comfort zone.

Know Your Community

It's important for therapists to know about community resources. Maintaining a list and updating it yearly is a good practice. Even better is being
part enough of the community so that you know: "Who is the sensitive
dentist to refer orally sexually abused patients to?" "What church or
synagogue is friendly to persons struggling with sexual identity and/or

transgender issues?" "Are there employers who have been willing to give the formerly psychiatrically disabled person a job and a chance?" "Who is the psychiatrist that is savvy about providing medication support to 'graduating' trauma survivors without trying to convince them that it was rapidly cycling bipolar disorder?" Unfortunately, there are many mental health and medical providers who do not work from a trauma-informed perspective, and who can confuse and hurt clients by trying to redefine and reconceptualize in unhelpful ways. It's important to try to direct clients away from these kinds of experiences, if possible. This sometimes requires subterranean knowledge. Which attending physician can help a person through an operation without their switching to alternate personalities? Which correctional officer in the prison is likely to attend and calm an upset patient rather than having them thrown into segregation? Which congregation and minister will not make this former prostitute feel deeply ashamed?

It is extraordinarily useful to build up a mental database of such helpers that can be shared with clients at the appropriate times. I used to know an auto mechanic who would fix old junkers for trauma clients without much money, and let them pay it off in time. Invaluable.

Common Countertransference Reactions and Struggles—Rebuilding a Life Phase

Complex trauma therapy is often hard and extended work. Even when and if things are going well, the length and demands, and the personal emotional costs to the therapist of going through the intense feelings of the grief and anger stages, can present special difficulties as the client moves towards the completion of the work. Following are some examples:

1. **Exhaustion**. Other than the high trajectory/fast-changing patient described by Kluft (R. P. Kluft, 1994) and enjoyed by all therapists, work with this population can be a slog. It takes time for the therapist to get taken into the client's psychological system and to be a counterweight to the childhood messages and core beliefs. Therapists can have a sense of "will this *ever end*???" And in truth, thera-

pists who are only gratified by quick success, or who are most comfortable simply "teaching skills" likely should not be working with this type of client.

a. Exhaustion is best handled by peer support and specialized consultation. This is daunting work to do in isolation and, in fact, it can be dangerous to client and therapist alike. Attending conferences, joining a complex-trauma therapist's support group, starting one of those if they don't exist, and engaging in active self-assessment and self-care are all ways to manage this issue. Learning tools may be had at www.isst-d.org. There is an active and very helpful listserv run by a former president of the International Society for the Study of Trauma and Dissociation, Dr. Rick Chefetz, that can be joined at www.dissoc.icors.org/.

2. **Boundary flexing**. Years of therapy have the effect of creating a deep and intimate relationship. When the client improves, it is flattering and satisfying for the therapist. You may find yourself feeling quasi-parental pride. You may also start pondering whether standard boundaries should still apply to the relationship with this client. When does this person get to be a full human being? Would it be wrong to go out for that cup of coffee? Or that lunch he or she has proposed? Or to ask advice on the office you are moving to or redecorating? Or to use them as your cleaning person or real estate broker, for example. There is a temptation to "validate" the client by becoming more like a friend. It *is* likely that there will be changes in the relationship. The client will not be so dependent and will begin to behave as a co-equal adult, rather than a client with little or no sense of personal strength. However, the changes the client has made, though hard earned, are fragile and subject to reversals. There will be recursions, perhaps other grief or anger work to do, perhaps a current life crisis. Therapists need to remain available in the therapist role now and in the future. The standard therapist-client relationship does become a bit less formal as the client changes and matures. But it is important to hold on to your therapist role skills and position lest there be recursions, new crises, or a break in the client's now higher functioning. Failure to maintain this balance in

the changing relationship can lead to the next possible relational countertransference struggle, premature termination.

3. **Premature termination**. Parallel to exhaustion and boundary flexing is the temptation to believe all the work is done without giving it time to stabilize and survive some real-world tests. It is again gratifying to think the client has gone through this terribly difficult journey with you; the two of you have "triumphed" over the adversities; the fledgling bird is ready to leave the nest. When considering termination, it is important to see the client through some challenges, to assess whether he or she maintains, whether he or she begins to coalesce a coherent sense of pride that allows them to stand up to the rigors of life. In this model, termination often does not look like the classic "picture in the book" of the intense working through of the meaning of the therapist-client relationship followed by the firm handshake and goodbye. It is more like—well, we have much more to say on termination in the next chapter.

4. **Role reversal**. Therapists who work with complex trauma are themselves often victims, or at least persons with extra measures of sensitivity and personal vulnerability. One does not go into this area of work for no reason. Therapists' lives have challenges (i.e., they face marital crises, health crises, problems with children or aging parents, or all of these). And here is this person, this soon-to-be ex-client, whom the therapist has been increasingly intimate with over years, a person you have seen grow, and who you have admired for the tremendous courage they have shown. Now they are becoming a fuller person. The therapist might be tempted to share personal issues with them. Would that be so wrong? Wouldn't it make them feel more equal? Sometimes it is important for the therapist to acknowledge that he or she is distracted by issues other than the client's. Sometimes it's unavoidable—if your leg's in a cast or you're now five months pregnant and showing—some discussion is needed and is often helpful in a way that clients do appreciate (C. Dalenberg, 2014; C. J. Dalenberg, 2000, 2004). The important point is not to make major changes to defined boundaries and/or fall into thinking along the lines of "Ms. X is now so special and healed we can be

friends. Or sexual partners." A further discussion of the sexual pulls follows.

5. **Sexuality**. Intimacy is sexy. We are biological animals. We are wired to have sexual feelings towards age-appropriate potential partners/mates. In the therapy room, the so-called eroticized transference is common and sometimes mutual, particularly if the therapist is in a time of personal crisis and vulnerability. In earlier years of psychotherapy, it was not uncommon for therapists to marry their former patients, many of whom had complex trauma in their histories. That has changed and all sexual contact between therapist and client is now unethical, according to the codes of the major professional organizations. Beyond the obvious reasons not to go there—that it is not good for the patient and may severely damage them by recapitulating their original abuse—it is not good for the therapist either and can result in the loss of license and livelihood, marriage and family, and community esteem, and in incarceration in some states, to name a few of the major ones. *Such transgressions within a trusting relationship creates betrayal and repeats abuse/exploitation by a powerful figure.* Sex between therapists and former clients makes it impossible for a person to ever return to the therapist for further work. It confuses selfless love, Agape, with Eros. It is also very hard to consider that powerful transference feelings towards the therapist can ever be totally worked through. The therapist was a central figure in the client's recovery, and the memories of all the child-like yearnings and wishes are not erased by the client's growth. Readers should not just dismiss this possibility out of hand. Interpersonal fields are strong, and we are fallible human beings. However, there are far more chances for this to go wrong than to go right. There is too little training of psychotherapists in these pulls; they are often ignored as if they do not exist and therapists are simply issued a "Don't do that!" command. There is an excellent book exploring this subject that readers are referred to and urged to examine, by Pope et. al. (K. S. Pope, Sonne, & Holroyd, 1993).

6. **Professional recruitment**. "Yes, Mr. X, you are so sensitive, of course you would make a fine therapist. I'd be happy to write you

that letter of recommendation to my graduate school." Again, this can be *so* flattering, after years of such hard work the client wants to emulate you! Is it really good for the client? Can they handle the terrible things they would likely have to hear? Can they avoid being triggered? Can they avoid assuming every patient is a trauma survivor? Can they avoid believing that doing therapy the way theirs was done is the only correct way? Can they manage the business side or are they so motivated to help that they would shortchange their own ability to make a living? Are their boundaries solid enough to avoid the pitfalls we have been talking about? And should we really be writing recommendations for our ex-clients?

7. **Co-writing/teaching**. Particularly if one has successfully helped their first long-term severe-abuse survivor patient, the temptation may be to go on the road, begin to conduct workshops, bring the patient with you, have them testify to the worth of your methods, something that may be hard to resist. Avoid it. It is exploitive of the patient and as a therapist you need a great deal more experience before teaching others. This also applies to the next issue, writing a book.

8. **Writing your own book**. A critical meme exists among historians for persons who do not do their own intense research in original sources: "Read ten books, write one." It likely takes a good deal of seasoning, with all the different attachment stances, over a significant number of years, to be ready to write your own book.

Notes on Dissociative Patients

A primary issue in the dissociative patient's increased and improved integration into the community is the extent of internal readiness and cohesion. If the therapist has avoided pushing away parts of the mind he/she did not feel comfortable working with, and has made sure that the entire system is "on board," this process proceeds more smoothly. Often, the desire to make better outside relationships can facilitate integration of certain parts of the mind. The internal cooperating teams of alter personalities created in prior therapy stages may spontaneously begin to blend together. Or, there may be a growing desire of certain alter states to merge. "Susie feels so close to the Protector that she wants to hold his hand/sit on his lap while we go to the library opening." Sometimes the alter personalities will ask themselves to have an experience of blending; other times it becomes obvious for the therapist to raise the question. Often, a successful merger of some parts will generate a desire from others to have that same feeling of becoming one with parts of the mind they are closest to. It is always important to ask whether there is internal resistance to such mergers or possible internal jealousy, and not to help with an integration ritual or experience until the internal agreements have been worked out. And, it is usually more successful for a more integrated and less unpredictable person to go out into the community looking for improved relationships than for a person that is still massively internally divided. Try to sense the readiness for closeness/merger and take the opportunities, once checking with other parts of the mind.

Summary and Major Points

1. If/when grief and anger processing have successfully occurred, movement towards more open involvement with life often happens naturally. Clinicians should monitor and recognize these movements and support them.
2. Aloneness and emptiness are a legacy of trauma but are not "reality." Survivors often seem to be wearing blinders and to not perceive opportunities that may be there for being in healthy, sustaining relationships with others. Encourage the growth of a wider field of view.
3. Recognize and encourage small openings in either perceptual changes of what is possible—"well I might try that garden club"— or overt behavior such as attending something new of interest.
4. Be aware of countertransference pulls towards friendship, sex, marriage, making the client a confidant, business partner, etc.
5. Do not use the years of work and responsibility and the client's progress as a rationalization to share elements of your own life in a way that is self-serving for you.

6. Continue to encourage association vs. dissociation. Encourage the client to approach rather than avoid difficult emotional material and life changes.

7. Make sure that the positive movements are shared by all parts of the dissociative system, if the client has a full-blown dissociative disorder. Continue to encourage internal alliances between remaining parts to move slowly and carefully farther into the outside world.

8. Use the growing closeness among internal parts to accomplish whatever level of integration the person is capable of as they increasingly re-engage with the external world.

13
PATTERNS OF TERMINATION

There are now two "classic" versions of termination, essentially arising out of the two major theoretical schools of therapy work. The more recent cognitive-behavioral paradigm generally would hold that the client goes through the prescribed treatment in the manual and the therapy ends after the six or ten or 15 visits called for by the typical cognitive-behavioral therapy (CBT) protocol. However, even there, it rarely looks like "the picture in the book." In supervising beginning psychotherapists in several professions, what often happens is that the CBT intervention is tried *as a component of therapy that then goes on, because there is some improvement but nothing like readiness for termination.* The CBT and/or EMDR interventions become a component of relational therapy. As the roiling, internal boil of unresolved trauma diminishes and the client-therapist relationship is taken in as a powerful competing metaphor for views of people, life, and possibilities, the client may become more responsive to skill development and better able to use it. Skills are learned and used within the context of a real healing relationship. Attempts to get clients to "just use their skills" have been doomed to failure in my experience with complex psychological trauma clients, and have often led to symptom escalation or therapy stasis. So, even the CBT narrative is rarely as it is described theoretically.

The more analytic/relational narrative would hold that as the client stabilizes, works through the traumas, and moves toward healthier views of self, world, and relationship, he or she begins to reach out further to the community. The need for the therapist drops off. There is a period of mutual reflection on the meaning of the work. There are sessions of intense processing of the feeling of loss and of gratitude by the patient, and often by a very touched and emotional therapist. They set a date, and then therapy ends, with an open door for return should troubles arise again.

In my experience, very few complex trauma therapies end this way. There are many reasons:

1. Unavoidable life changes. The therapist changes jobs, moves, has a health crisis.
2. Unavoidable life changes. The client changes jobs, moves, has a health crisis.
3. Funding problems. The insurance company will not pay any more and the client can't. This is a huge ethical bind that therapists should think through ahead of time. This can lead to major countertransference resentment of the client if the fee is set too low; therefore, it is inadvisable to continue a therapy without discussing financial means in detail, and it is advisable for the therapist (especially one in private practice) to set a fee that is based on his or her business model and not just on the needs of the client. How many pro bono or $5.00 an hour clients can a therapist carry?
4. Natural growth. At the beginning, the therapy is often all-consuming for the client. Nothing in life is more important than getting to those hours. The client hangs with his/her fingernails to a cliff, until the next contact. Any interruption in the schedule, be it therapist vacations, holidays, or conference attendance, can create a crisis. These events require very careful backup arrangements, and sometimes telephone contact during times away. The dependency of the most common attachment type, the insecure/ambivalent/preoccupied client, is intense. Over the years, the goal is for this to change and for the client to develop a satisfying life apart from the treatment. The importance of the therapy hours starts to move down the hierarchy of wants and needs. Life becomes more important than therapy, and isn't *this* a great victory?

This growth of actual life involvement leads to what I have experienced as the most common pattern of termination, the drifting away pattern. In that pattern, gradually, the client's attendance changes. There is an occasional cancellation when the client has something more important to do—hallelujah! The client's social network expands, leaving less time for and focus on the therapy. Hours of emptiness are often replaced by expanded job possibilities, community volunteering, occupational changes, school attendance. As this happens, the treatment contract can be renegotiated. Often, it moves from a usual twice weekly an hour or more sessions to once a week, and then, maybe even every other week. You as the therapist and the therapy itself are no longer the major foci of the client's life. So, at some point you consciously acknowledge this and set a termination date—or this never gets done—but the client, now much better, moves to Alaska or Paris or Detroit. There is occasional contact of the "hi, this is how I'm doing" variety. Eventually contact stops. This is the pattern that has most characterized my relational therapy work with complex trauma survivors. There is rarely the satisfaction of the extended tender goodbye, but there is always the quiet internal glow of knowing a person is out there doing life and feeling much better. Although it is likely preferable to conduct the planned termination, and to ensure that no constellations of unresolved transference feelings result in the drifting away, this is just not always possible.

The last pattern is the most painful and difficult for the therapist, and maybe for the client also. Separation/individuation from parents is often conflicted and difficult, as anyone who has raised children has likely experienced. Not all kids grow up, go off to college, do fine, move out into the employment world, find a spouse/partner, and establish their own family and career. Likely this straight-through, without problems path is the *unusual*, given the fact that about 50% of students beginning college do not graduate within five years. In some families, and some therapies, the child/client storms off in anger. It is one way of breaking the intense bonds with the parent and with the therapist.

I have had the experience of helping a very self-critical and obsessive patient learn to let up on himself, and on his counter-phobic periods of explosive rebellion. The client became more self-compassionate and kinder to himself in his internal thought and feeling world. He was getting ready for a life change that would involve a move. Rather than processing the loss of the therapy, the client began to be highly critical and blaming of me, and eventually stormed off furious. The client felt that somehow I had "robbed him of his progress" before the client moved away. I was seen once again as a denying and critical person/ internal object. Of course, having the therapy end in this way was hurtful to me. One saving grace was that I heard from mutual contacts that after storming away, the client functioned better in his chosen occupation and within his social network. This pattern is now termed "storming off but being better." It is analogous to adolescent rebellion in service of self-differentiation.

The Process of Termination

The goal, of course, is to "put ourselves out of business"—in other words, to make it possible for the client to function independently as much as possible, without the need for continued therapy, though, of course, this need may re-emerge at a later time.

How do we get there? What are the signs that therapy for this client is ready to end?

A major determinant is whether the major traumas have been worked through, and that there has been generalization, along the previously described learning principles, from the actively worked traumas to those that don't necessarily need conscious processing. A trauma is "worked through" when the client has felt the feelings associated with the original traumatic event and perceived him/herself as moving through said event in temporal terms, so it now feels like the trauma is in the past and no longer has the "right now" flashback-like quality. It has become "just a memory." Whether one uses EMDR, fractionated abreactions, or some of the other trauma-processing methods in Chapters 10 and 11 describing phases on working through, there is a distinct change in the affect expressed and in the room once a trauma is worked through.

To try to capture this change in imagery, at the beginning of the trauma work we have the tempest of hurt, rage, self-blame, and betrayal feelings—truly a foggy, dangerous, stormy river. As the client moves forward through the storm and out the other side, the river opens up, it is sunnier, the storm clouds have receded. A distinct sense of coming through to a more peaceful place occurs.

Even if one does not use a formal EMDR protocol, it is crucial to have an idea of how the nature of the world looks to the client as working through occurs, and often to describe the "states of the river" while the client moves forward through the traumatic experience. Permissive hypnosis is again an enormously powerful tool. . . . "Your mind will know just the right peaceful place for you to rest and care for yourself after this journey." It is essential to move forward through time. The idea is *not* to make the client re-experience every trauma they have had, but to help them move through and leave behind a particular experience that is often then generalized to similar situations.

In dissociative patients, this process leads towards natural integration and/or planned integrations.

Notes on Dissociative Patients

What is integration for clients with major dissociative disorders? How does a person get there? Is it desirable for every client? Obtainable?

I have seen two patterns of integration, often experienced by the same patient. The natural growth pattern looks like a coalescing of internal alliances in which the perceived separate parts agree to go through trauma processing together; a shared sense of alliance between some parts already exists, previously encouraged and built by the therapist/client dyad. So, "the baby, the big sister, the punisher/protector have agreed to hold hands as they go through the grief about x together." Once that grief process has been done, often a felt melting/blending occurs. It is most specifically *not* a disappearance, but a desired melding. "The baby doesn't want to be all alone anymore and is just wanting to be inside/with the protector now that he is acting nice." The impetus does not come from the therapist, but by the dissolving of internal amnestic and functional barriers and the resolution of internal conflict that no longer feel "right" or "needed" by the client. Sometimes, after a period of working through, the therapist will ask about a particular alter or set of alters only to hear "oh, they just blended in after we talked about x." This is my favorite way for an integration to take place—a natural process of felt barriers no longer being necessary and self-dissolving.

When clients express fear of important parts disappearing, there is another "bakery analogy" that is useful. When integration works well, no parts disappear; they simply contribute who/what they are, and their skills, to a whole. They become like marble cheesecake.

The various parts contribute to the "flavor of the whole." The sense of separateness often but not always goes; the skills and qualities of the parts become accessible to the whole person. So, "persecutor/protector, how would it feel to actually have your power and ability to protect available all the time?" "Kid sister, what about having your life and playfulness available to the whole human being?" And so forth. In the cases processed in this manner, clients have not expressed feelings of loss of separateness, but of gains of internal friendship, caring, cooperation and dramatically improved functional abilities. In general, integration should be additive, not subtractive.

Directed Integration

No one who has not trained thoroughly in dissociative disorder therapy and in hypnosis should try to perform a directed integration. Those wanting to develop the knowledge and skills needed are again referred to the training workshops put on jointly by the International Society for the Study of Trauma and Dissociation and the American Society of Clinical Hypnosis. The following description is what a directed integration might look and sound like.

"John and Susan and the baby have been growing very close. They have said that they miss being with each other and want to be together all the time. They have agreed to blend their energies and to become one part of the whole human being. Now let's check if each of those parts of the mind is still feeling that way—can they say how this idea is feeling for them? (Check with parts.) Are there other parts of the mind that are not in favor of this, or are threatened by it? Are there parts that hope to subvert this or prevent it? Let's check with the parts of the mind. (Ask for objections; if they exist, work on these, not on the integration: 'OK, we need to postpone this till it is OK with everyone.') OK, now that all parts of the mind agree, or have said it does not matter and they do not want to pay attention or object to it, let's go ahead."

"We decided a while ago that John and Susan would hold hands and they would both cradle the baby. Let's ask them to sit together in just the right way; your mind will know what that is. Now let John and Susan join hands underneath the baby. Feel John and Susan's energy begin to blend together, and to take in the peaceful and loving energy of the baby. Feel the energy of one pour into the energy of the other. Feel them getting closer and closer to each other till all the energy is one, pouring and mixing and giving a sense of peace and unity to the whole. Let this mixing and blending and tender hugging and coming together keep moving forward. Let it continue till I count to ten; with each number the blending and closeness grows until there is no sense of separateness left. And now, as we reach ten, you may open your eyes as you are ready and tell me how that feels now inside."

Termination in the Three Cases

We have previously discussed Laurie, our insecure/ambivalent/pre-occupied client with DID who came to realize that we were talking about the "normal person problems" she had wanted to focus on at the beginning of the therapy, many years before. How did this therapy end? Shortly after the "normal person problems" realization, Laurie came into a session and described that all her internal parts had melded, some naturally, some through chosen integration exercises/processing. She now said that the only part remaining was the smallest, undamaged baby self. Laurie's felt-experience was that this part was too precious, a pre-trauma whole, core of self, to become integrated. She expressed it by saying, "I think the best we are going to be able to do is Siamese twins." The smallest baby part was to be joined with but also separate from the rest of the whole person. I asked whether this worked for her, and she affirmed that it felt right. We then began to stretch the sessions out—first once a week, then once every other week, once in three weeks, once a month, and then after some months, stopping. After this, there were a few sessions with Laurie's son to discuss practical parenting/school issues. I made the judgment that knowing huge amounts of material about the family trumped the boundary stretch of doing this, and it did not lead to problems. After that, long periods of no contact occurred, with my eventually moving from the town in which the therapy occurred.

At termination and afterwards, clients do not then go on to lead perfect stress-less lives, and some have a need to re-engage in treatment. Some years after the termination and my move, Laurie called and asked whether she could return to therapy, despite the long drive this would entail. This is where therapist self-examination becomes crucial. It became clear to me, after conducting an "internal check," that I had given all I had to give and was too close to retirement to restart this therapy. I discussed this with the client, and a careful referral was made. She moved on to work on whatever the new problem focus was with someone else.

Frank, our chaotic client, drifted away. After the integration dream, he began to work much more seriously on his addiction struggles. He gradually dropped the chaotic rebellion/reconnection pattern with his wife. He began to attend work more regularly and keep his scheduled repair appointments. And like many people who view their therapist in the same metaphor as their primary care physician, his "psychological flu" was better and he did not need more appointments, and he went back into his life functioning better. There has been no further contact.

Roberta lowered her expectations for a life partner, choosing to stay with the devoted but less than interpersonally compelling engineer. They had two children. This termination was complex, because Roberta traveled in social circles in which I and my family members were also involved. Perhaps this is avoidable in big cities. In rural practice, it is not rare. It was crucial here that the therapist maintain boundaries between what transpired in the therapy and the client in the outside world. The attitude was and had to be that Roberta was a fully functional adult and whatever I knew of her did not inform my interactions within the social circles that we both frequented. Some of my obvious weaknesses, shyness, and self-doubt in the larger world beyond the therapy room were actually helpful for Roberta to experience because they allowed her to feel co-equal. It was true, as Harry Stack Sullivan said, that we are all human beings and all more or less the same (Sullivan, 1938).

Getting Introjected Metaphors

A relational prerequisite for termination is that somehow, the therapist as a countervailing presence to the abuser(s), must get taken in. The therapist must become strongly present within the client's internal world, a supportive part of the Greek chorus we all carry within our minds observing and commenting on what we do. There is no shortcut to this; it develops as we go through crises and formal periods of working through traumas with our clients. There is no substitute for actually having been there when another human being needed you. In complex trauma cases, this must happen over and over and over until the client can depend on it/you. I have found no substitute for persistence and patience.

However, it's also important to think of methods to consciously and directly try to hasten this sense in the client and consciously try to build it. One client came up with a lovely metaphor. She always wanted the experience of being held and rocked by her mother, who had died of disease early in her life. While we were in the working-through phase, the client made herself a "transitional object." She obtained a dollhouse–sized rocking chair. She made little straw-stuffed mommy and baby dolls. She put the baby doll in the mommy's lap. She brought it in and asked whether it might live on the mantelpiece of my office for a time. Remembering how often complex trauma survivors live in trance logic and magical thinking, and knowing how often a rock, even a business card from the therapist's office, is used as a talisman of connection, I agreed. The rocking chair "absorbed" whatever relational magic it needed, was taken home, and remained comforting. This can, of course, be done with any object, but the metaphor of the properly taken care of baby was crucial for this client, and has worked when suggested to other clients who have made their own kind of mother-baby caring object.

Stuffed animals can "obtain" this kind of magic when brought back and forth to therapy, but there must be an active process of weaning the patient from needing to carry one throughout life. Most jobs don't allow the police officer or clerk or lawyer or professor to carry their stuffed animal with them.

The metaphor of the therapist sitting on the client's shoulder often occurs naturally and can be encouraged and used. Clients will sometimes say, "I heard your voice as I was about to . . . go with that jerk, ignore my sense of danger, accept that I was only good for sex," etc. There's a balance between being narcissistic in describing the therapist on the shoulder and the realization that this is often a natural process. "What have we said here that has helped in the past" can be a useful probe because it incorporates sense data, listened-to speech. And sometimes "what might I say if I were sitting on your shoulder" seems useful and unavoidable. The client gets practice in remembering and using the interpretations and supports of the therapy.

Of course, this is also a time when skill-building is often most effective. Techniques that were felt to have secondary importance or not to be relevant when the client was in continual crisis become valuable tools here. This is the time when complex trauma clients can most often use dialectical behavior therapy (DBT) successfully. There is an internal structure and basis for using the skills, something to attach them to, a foundation. And as we have been saying all along, that foundation is the real relationship built between therapist and client over periods of struggle and coming through hard times together without broken bonds.

Common Countertransference Struggles—Termination Phase

Not Letting Go

No one is ever "all fixed." Life throws continual challenges, whether in relationships, jobs, health, finances, children, aging parents, or all combinations of these. It is sometimes a characteristic of therapists not to want to discuss termination until the client is achieving optimum functioning, rather than just "good enough for them" functioning. We need to let the client enter or re-enter the world and cope with hurdles, returning when and if they need—which is the best reason not to pursue friendship.

Friendship, Once Again

Sometimes, maybe even often, the most admirable people we have contact with are our clients. We work with them through life-threatening struggles. We admire their enormous courage. We stand in awe of what they have survived, their potential after substantial healing, their talent. We have spent years getting and feeling close and it is not a phony closeness. Two people who have gone through the intense grief and scorching anger of the middle phase of treatment have a bond of shared intense, difficult, productive, rewarding, experience. If it were armed combat, we would expect the development of that feeling veterans often call "comradeship." It is natural to want this to continue. And sometimes doing so validates for the patient that he or she is a fully equal human being. The down side is that moving to friendship may mask unresolved transference feelings, prolong dependency in different garb, and remove a potential future resource from the client's likely still small group of people they can depend on in a crisis. It is also questionable whether the power imbalance between therapist and client can ever be really overcome, and whether this always places the potential former client "friend" in a sometimes unconscious one-down position. When I have allowed the very warm feelings to develop into friendship, somewhere later along the way it became clear that the therapist up/client down positions were never fully relinquished, despite great efforts on both sides. I have tried to allow mutual friendships with an extraordinary client or two. They were, in fact, some of the most admirable people I have ever known. But, it always turned out that somewhere along the way, the power imbalance was still there, interfered with real equality, and left somewhat stung fingers on both sides. In retrospect, perhaps it was unwise to try.

It is also important to remember that the therapy relationship is unique in being *both real and idealized at the same time*. Hopefully our clients see us at our best. We are not expected to show them our irritability if the morning did not go right, our possible withdrawal from family after "giving so much at the office," or the neurotic self-doubt we may share with our own therapist. As these things become more easily known if the therapist tries to enter friend mode, the crash from the pedestal can be hard, and I think it damages the work that has already been done. When clients maintain a quasi-ideal view of the therapist, as they often do, this confers on the therapist the right and the ability to do the mirroring functioning Kohut talks about, and to *be* the idealized object that the client needs (R. P. Kluft, Kinsler, & O'Neil, 2014; Kohut & Wolf, 1992). This is not a position to abandon without great care.

Boundary Breaking

As past chair of a State Psychology Licensing Board, I have seen multiple instances of therapeutic closeness develop into exploitive sexual or financial relationships—from hiring a client to clean the office, leading to business disputes; to renting office space to a client, leading to landlord-tenant disputes; to alleged barter arrangements, leading therapists to exploit clients in performing child care; to sex, resulting in multiple losses, including marriages that fall apart.

Unfortunately, marginalized groups have also tended to feel that maintaining boundaries does not apply to their group because of their uniqueness—"we are the only two Tasmanian LGBT persons in the whole area; it was fate that we found each other." These relationships regularly blow up, and can lead to horrendous consequences, including legal action, for everyone involved. The intensity of the transference and countertransference feelings do not disappear when persons are of a "special, unique" category. In fact, the feelings might be intensified and may be what lead to transgressions in the first place.

Acquiring an Acolyte

Here, the admiration the client feels for the therapist gets expressed by the client adopting and advocating for the unique expertise and specialness of their therapist, and proselytizing for them and the theory from which they operate. They may become therapists who religiously study and practice within the same "school of thought" of the therapist. They may become walking advertisements for the therapist's speaking engagements or conference presentations. They may and do offer to go on speaking engagements with the therapist to talk about how Dr. X "cured" them. These instances maintain the therapist in an one-up position and the current or former patient in a one-down position and can lead to exploitation. The therapist and "cured" client might, for example, propose a mutual presentation at professional conferences; this too is against the parameters of professional codes of ethics.

Self-Aggrandizement and Premature Expertise

Let me first plead guilty to this one, and then explain it. It is enormously gratifying to successfully work with one's first highly challenging complex trauma and/or dissociative patient. In doing so, one almost has to be creative, expand what one has been taught in school, and make it through harrowing suicidal or other crises. An outcome of such an experience is to believe that what you have discovered is so unique and special that it requires a book and nationwide speaking tour. Although there is no doubt that early career professionals have a lot to offer in thinking and writing theoretically and practically, it is also likely wise to clinically test those ideas over a greater number of clients and years, and to compare and contrast techniques with what others have learned for some external validation. It makes for a more sober and more seasoned clinician (and workshop presenter!).

This type of mistake might come under the heading of therapist over-involvement and some grandiosity.

Sudden Inflexible Boundary Imposition or Relational Withdrawal

As this book has emphasized, the healing is in the relationship, making it crucial not to destroy the work through sudden rigidity and coldness of boundaries. Sometimes, as termination approaches, therapists may be reminded of "how it should be done," "what the masters have taught us." There may be an internal "oh dear, I've moved too far away from my theories" self-observation and criticism in the therapist's mind. So, one more story about myself:

> I had attended a psychoanalytically focused conference and had once again gotten pulled into believing that a neutral, inquiring relational stance was the way to go. I returned to a very bright college-aged patient, and I suppose in my most pompous

imagining I was channeling Freud's voice, asked her "So, what is it you feel I represent to you?" She virtually cracked up and responded, "Oh, c'mon, you know you're the kind father I never had—now can we go back to doing therapy?"

So let's not end the work by destroying the closeness we have worked so hard to develop. Following are some additional common mistakes.

Avoidance of Discussing Termination

Goodbyes are hard. It's easy not to do them. Why bring up what may make you, the therapist, sad, or induce sadness in the client? Why not just let them drift off without processing attempts? The clearest reason for this is that doing so can prevent the client from feeling fully grown-up. It can maintain a fantasy of remaining in a child-like relationship to the therapist. It can prevent the client's feeling internally separate and OK. Hard as it is, we want the client to go off into his/her own life and to feel grown up, and it is the process of discussing the ending that helps accomplish this. Even within the drifting-away pattern, there can be a time to note and surface the issue, and do honor to the relationship you have had, even as it changes.

Notes on Termination With Dissociative Clients

As we have been saying, everything is more complex with dissociative clients. In the termination phase, it is particularly important to investigate the readiness of the entire self-system to terminate. Are there parts of a persecutor/protector personality that the person is keeping in reserve? Are there parts still bonded in ways to the abuser(s)? Inquire of the whole system whether integration is real or there are internal insurance policies. Ask for formerly individual parts of the mind to come forward should they still have feelings of separateness. Make sure, if a person has not fully integrated, that the internal alliances and configuration of the system is working well for the client and appears stable. If not, why not? Ask what there is left to work through. It may be necessary here to cycle back to instances of grief and anger that have not been processed. This is one of the places that the therapy can be recursive.

If necessary, do the grief and anger work for remaining alter personalities. Then give the client some time to see how this has all settled in and, if possible, weather through a crisis or two with them to see if the cohesion comes apart. If so, work again on the necessary internal alliances, grief, and anger work. "OK, let's go back and see what it is that's leaving Suzie stuck." Over sometimes several recursions, you and the client reach a place where poking at the prior sensitive spots no longer hurts, no longer leads to dissociation. They are "just memories." They become "no big deal" in the sense that they are no longer destabilizing. The client acquires a sense of "that was long ago, this is now." The same emotion-driven, over-aroused, limbic system–based reactions do not occur. The client can talk about past traumas in a more neutral voice. At that point, movement towards termination becomes natural as the person's social world continues to expand. It is then possible and necessary to speak of the grief and pride of letting go of the therapy.

Summary

Therapy of complex chronic-abuse survivors depends on a healing relationship as a major tool. It is impossible not to have a relationship with the client, regardless of what techniques are used. That relationship is responsible for much of therapeutic change, as discussed previously, in the review of psychotherapy outcome studies. Techniques work only within relationship.

The quality of the meta-messages we send is crucial to the client's healing. The over-arching meta-message is an anti-shame one. "You are worthy of respect and pride." Introjection of that view of self and world changes a client's internal feelings and external behaviors. In turn, the changed external behaviors, and the way the client holds him/herself out to the world, produce a more satisfying life for the client, and a quiet sense of shared pride in the therapist.

REFERENCES

Ainsworth, M. D. (1969). Object relations, dependency, and attachment: A theoretical review of the infant-mother relationship. *Child Development*, *40*(4), 969–1025. doi:10.2307/1127008

Ainsworth, M. D., Bell, S. M., & Stayton, D. J. (1972). Individual differences in the development of some attachment behaviors. *Merrill-Palmer Quarterly*, *18*(2), 123–143.

Ainsworth, M. D., & Gewitz, J. L. (1972). *Attachment and dependency: A comparison.* Oxford, England: V. H. Winston & Sons.

Ainsworth, M. D. S., Bell, S. M., & Stayton, D. F. (1974). Infant–mother attachment and social development: Socialization as a product of reciprocal responsiveness to signals. In M. P. M. Richards (Ed.), *The integration of a child into a social world* (pp. 99–135). New York, NY: Cambridge University Press.

Ainsworth, M. D. S., Blehar, M. C., Waters, E., & Wall, S. (1978). *Patterns of attachment: A psychological study of the strange situation.* Oxford, England: Lawrence Erlbaum.

Ainsworth, M. D. S., & Eichberg, C. G. (1991). Effects on infant–mother attachment of mother's unresolved loss of an attachment figure, or other traumatic experience. In C. M. Parkes, J. Stevenson-Hinde, & P. Marris (Eds.), *Attachment across the life cycle* (pp. 160–183). New York, NY: Tavistock/Routledge.

Ainsworth, M. S. (1979). Infant–mother attachment. *American Psychologist*, *34*(10), 932–937. doi:10.1037/0003-066X.34.10.932

American Psychiatric Association. (2000). *Diagnostic and statistical manual of mental disorders, fourth edition, text revision (DSM-IV-TR)*.

American Psychiatric Association. (2013). *Diagnostic and statistical manual of mental disorders: DSM-5*. Washington, DC: Author.

American Psychological Association. (2002). Ethical principles of psychologists and code of conduct. *American Psychologist*, *57*(12), 1060–1073.

American Psychological Association. (2010). 2010 amendments to the 2002 "Ethical principles of psychologists and code of conduct". *American Psychologist*, *65*(5), 493. http://dx.doi.org/10.1037/a0020168

American Psychological Association. (2011). American Psychological Association Committee on the Revision of the Specialty Guidelines for Forensic Psychology. *Specialty guidelines for forensic psychology*. Washington, DC: Author.

American Psychological Association. (2013). Recognition of psychotherapy effectiveness. *Journal of Psychotherapy Integration*, *23*(3), 320–330. Washington, DC: Author. http://dx.doi.org/10.1037/a0033179

Bandura, A., & Barab, P. G. (1971). Conditions governing nonreinforced imitation. *Developmental Psychology*, *5*(2), 244–255. doi:10.1037/h0031499

Bandura, A., Ross, D., & Ross, S. A. (1963). Vicarious reinforcement and imitative learning. *The Journal of Abnormal and Social Psychology*, *67*(6), 601–607. doi:10.1037/h0045550

Bandura, A., & Walters, R. H. (1963). *Social learning and personality development*. New York: Holt Rinehart and Winston.

Bazhenova, O. V., Stroganova, T. A., Doussard-Roosevelt, J. A., Posikera, I. A., & Porges, S. W. (2007). Physiological responses of 5-month-old infants to smiling and blank faces [Press release]. Retrieved from www.ncbi.nlm.nih.gov/pmc/articles/PMC1790728/pdf/nihms16211.pdf

Benson, H. (2000). *The relaxation response*. New York, NY: William Morris.

Bergin, A. E., & Strupp, H. H. (1970). The directions in psychotherapy research. *Journal of Abnormal Psychology*, *76*(1), 13–26. doi:10.1037/h0029634

Bohart, A. C., & Tallman, K. (2010). Clients: The neglected common factor in psychotherapy. In B. L. Duncan, S. D. Miller, B. E. Wampold, & M. A. Hubble (Eds.), *The heart and soul of change: Delivering what works in therapy (2nd ed.)* (pp. 83–111). Washington, DC: American Psychological Association. http://dx.doi.org/10.1037/12075-000

Bowlby, J. (1978). Attachment theory and its therapeutic implications. *Adolescent Psychiatry, 6*, 5–33.

Bowlby, J. (1980). *Attachment and loss*. New York, NY: Basic Books.

Bowlby, J. (1983). Attachment and loss: Retrospect and prospect. *Annual Progress in Child Psychiatry & Child Development*, 29–47.

Bowlby, J. (1986). The nature of the child's tie to his mother. In P. Buckley (Ed.), *Essential papers on object relations* (pp. 153–199). New York, NY: New York University Press.

Bowlby, J. (1988). *A secure base: Parent-child attachment and healthy human development*. New York, NY: Basic Books.

Bowlby, J. (1989). The role of attachment in personality development and psychopathology. In S. I. Greenspan & G. H. Pollock (Eds.), *The course of life, Vol. 1: Infancy* (pp. 229–270). Madison, CT: International Universities Press, Inc.

Bowlby, R. (2004). *Fifty years of attachment theory*. London, England: Karnac Books.

Boxer, P., & Terranova, A. M. (2008). Effects of multiple maltreatment experiences among psychiatrically hospitalized youth. *Child Abuse & Neglect, 32*(6), 637–647. doi:10.1016/j.chiabu.2008.02.003

Bradley, R., Jenei, J., & Westen, D. (2005). Etiology of borderline personality disorder: Disentangling the contributions of intercorrelated antecedents. *Journal of Nervous and Mental Disease, 193*(1), 24–31. doi:10.1097/01.nmd.0000149215.88020.7c

Brand, B. L., McNary, S. W., Myrick, A. C., Classen, C. C., Lanius, R., Loewenstein, R. J., Pain, C., & Putnam, F. W. (2012). A longitudinal naturalistic study of patients with dissociative disorders treated by community clinicians. *Psychological Trauma: Theory, Research, Practice, and Policy, 5*(4), 301–308. http://dx.doi.org/10.1037/a0027654

Brenneis, C. B. (1997). Final report of APA working group on investigation of memories of childhood abuse: A critical commentary. *Psychoanalytic Psychology, 14*(4), 531–547. http://dx.doi.org/10,1037/h0085224

Bromberg, P. M. (2003). Something wicked this way comes: Trauma, dissociation, and conflict: The space where psychoanalysis, cognitive science, and neuroscience overlap. *Psychoanalytic Psychology, 20*(3), 558–574. doi:10.1037/0736-9735.20.3.558

Bromberg, P. M. (2006). *Awakening the dreamer: Clinical journeys.* Mahwah, NJ: Analytic Press.

Bromberg, P. M. (2008). "Mentalize this!" dissociation, enactment, and clinical process. In E. L. Jurist, A. Slade, & S. Bergner (Eds.), *Mind to mind: Infant research, neuroscience, and psychoanalysis* (pp. 414–434). New York, NY: Other Press.

Bromberg, P. M. (2009). Multiple self-states, the relational mind, and dissociation: A psychoanalytic perspective. In P. F. Dell & J. A. O'Neil (Eds.), *Dissociation and the dissociative disorders: DSM-V and beyond* (pp. 637–652). New York, NY: Routledge/Taylor & Francis Group.

Bromberg, P. M. (2013). Hidden in plain sight: Thoughts on imagination and the lived unconscious. *Psychoanalytic Dialogues, 23*(1), 1–14. doi:10.1080/10481885.2013.754275

Bromberg, P. M. (2014). Sullivan as pragmatic visionary: Operationalist and oper relationalist. *Contemporary Psychoanalysis, 50*(4), 509–530. doi:10.1080/00107530.2014.942588

Bromberg, P. M. (2016). It never entered my mind. In E. F. Howell & S. Itzkowitz (Eds.), *The dissociative mind in psychoanalysis: Understanding and working with trauma* (pp. 118–126). New York, NY: Routledge/Taylor & Francis Group.

Campbell, L. F., Norcross, J. C., Vasquez, M. J. T., & Kaslow, N. J. (2013). Recognition of psychotherapy effectiveness: The APA resolution. *Psychotherapy, 50*(1), 98–101. doi:10.1037/a0031817

Carkhuff, R. R. (1969). Critical variables in effective counselor training. *Journal of Counseling Psychology, 16*(3), 238–245. doi:10.1037/h0027223

Carkhuff, R. R., Kratochvil, D., & Friel, T. (1968). Efects of professional training: Communication and discrimination of facilitative conditions. *Journal of Counseling Psychology, 15*(1), 68–74. doi:10.1037/h0025258

Carkhuff, R. R., & Truax, C. B. (1965). Training in counseling and psychotherapy: An evaluation of an integrated didactic and experiential approach. *Journal of Consulting Psychology, 29*(4), 333–336. doi:10.1037/h0022187

Carkhuff, R. R., & Truax, C. B. (1966). Toward explaining success and failure in interpersonal learning experiences. *Personnel & Guidance Journal, 44*(7), 723–728. doi:10.1002/j.2164-4918.1966.tb03856.x

Carlson, E. B., & Dalenberg, C. J. (2000). A conceptual framework for the impact of traumatic experiences. *Trauma, Violence, & Abuse, 1*(1), 4–28. doi:10.1177/1524838000001001002

Carlson, E. B., Dalenberg, C. J., Armstrong, J., Daniels, J. W., Loewenstein, R., & Roth, D. (2001). Multivariate prediction of posttraumatic symptoms in psychiatric inpatients. *Journal of Traumatic Stress, 14*(3), 549–567. doi:10.1023/a:1011164707774

Ceci, S. J., & Bruck, M. (1995). *Jeopardy in the courtroom: A scientific analysis of children's testimony.* Washington, DC: American Psychological Association. http://dx.doi.org/10.1037/10180-000

Ceci, S. J., Huffman, M. L. C., Smith, E., & Loftus, E. F. (1994). Repeatedly thinking about a non-event: Source misattributions among preschoolers. *Consciousness and Cognition: An International Journal, 3*(3–4), 388–407. doi:10.1006/ccog.1994.1022

Ceci, S. J., Huffman, M. L. C., Smith, E., & Loftus, E. F. (1996). Repeatedly thinking about a non-event: Source misattributions among preschoolers. In K. E. Pezdek & W. P. Banks (Eds.), *The recovered memory/false memory debate* (pp. 225–244). San Diego, CA: Academic Press.

Ceci, S. J., & Loftus, E. F. (1994). "Memory work": A royal road to false memories? *Applied Cognitive Psychology, 8*(4), 351–364. doi:10.1002/acp.2350080405

Chalavi, S., Vissia, E. M., Giesen, M. E., Nijenhuis, E. R. S., Draijer, N., Cole, J. H., . . . Reinders, A. A. T. S. (2015). Abnormal hippocampal morphology in dissociative identity disorder and posttraumatic stress disorder correlates with childhood trauma and dissociative symptoms. *Human Brain Mapping, 36*(5), 1692–1704. doi:10.1002/hbm.22730

Chu, J., Dell. P. F., Van der Hart, O., Cardeña, E., Barach, P. M., Somer, E., . . . Twombly, J. (2011). Guidelines for treating dissociative identity disorder in adults, third revision. *Journal of Trauma & Dissociation, 12*, 115–187.

Cloitre, M., Courtois, C. A., Charuvastra, A., Carapezza, R., Stolbach, B. C., & Green, B. L. (2011). Treatment of complex PTSD: Results of the ISTSS expert clinician survey on best practices. *Journal of Traumatic Stress, 24*(6), 615–627. doi:10.1002/jts.20697

Cloitre, M., Courtois, C. A., Ford, J. D., Green, B. L., Alexander, P., Briere, J., . . . Van der Hart, O. (2012). The ISTSS expert consensus treatment guidelines for complex PTSD in adults. Retrieved from http://www.istss.org/[.6/3/2017

Cloitre, M., Stolbach, B. C., Herman, J. L., van der Kolk, B., Pynoos, R., Wang, J., & Petkova, E. (2009). A developmental approach to complex PTSD: Childhood and adult cumulative trauma as predictors of symptom complexity. *Journal of Traumatic Stress, 22*(5), 399–408. doi:10.1002/jts.20444

Courtois, C. A. (1997a). Delayed memories of child sexual abuse: Critique of the controversy and clinical guidelines. In M. A. Conway (Ed.), *Recovered memories and false memories* (pp. 206–229). New York, NY: Oxford University Press. http://dx.doi.org/10.1093/med:psych/9780198523864.003.0009

Courtois, C. A. (1997b). Guidelines for the treatment of adults abused or possibly abused as children (with attention to issues of delayed/recovered memory). *American Journal of Psychotherapy, 51*(4), 497–510.

Courtois, C. A. (1999). *Recollections of sexual abuse: Treatment principles and guidelines.* New York, NY: W. W. Norton & Co.

Courtois, C. A. (2001). Implications of the memory controversy for clinical practice: An overview of treatment recommendations and guidelines [Press release]. Retrieved from www.tandfonline.com/doi/abs/10.1300/J070v09n03_09

Courtois, C. A. (2004). Complex trauma, complex reactions: Assessment and treatment. *Psychotherapy: Theory, Research, Practice, Training, 41*(4), 412–425. doi:10.1037/0033-3204.41.4.412

Courtois, C. A. (2010). *Healing the incest wound: Adult survivors in therapy (2nd ed.)*. New York, NY: W. W. Norton & Co.

Courtois, C. A. (2012). Retraumatization and complex traumatic stress: A treatment overview. In M. P. Duckworth & V. M. Follette (Eds.), *Retraumatization: Assessment, treatment, and prevention* (pp. 163–190). New York, NY: Routledge/Taylor & Francis Group.

Courtois, C. A., & Ford, J. D. (2009). *Treating complex traumatic stress disorders: An evidence based guide*. New York, NY: Guilford Press.

Courtois, C. A., & Ford, J. D. (2013). *Treatment of complex trauma: A sequenced, relationship-based approach*. New York, NY: Guilford Press.

Dalenberg, C. (2014). *Plenary Address: Countertransference and Transference Crises in Working with Traumatized Patients*. Paper presented at the ISSTD International Conference, Long Beach, CA.

Dalenberg, C. J. (1994). Making and finding memories: A commentary on the "repressed memory" controversy. *Journal of Child Sexual Abuse: Research, Treatment, & Program Innovations for Victims, Survivors, & Offenders, 3*(3), 109–118. doi:10.1300/J070v03n03_08

Dalenberg, C. J. (2000). The argument for highlighting, examining, and disclosing countertransference in trauma therapy. In C. J. Dalenberg (Ed.), *Countertransference and the treatment of trauma* (pp. 23–56). Washington, DC: American Psychological Association. http://dx.doi.org/10.1037/10380-002.

Dalenberg, C. J. (2004). Maintaining the safe and effective therapeutic relationship in the context of distrust and anger: Countertransference and complex trauma. *Psychotherapy: Theory, Research, Practice, Training, 41*(4), 438–447. doi:10.1037/0033-3204.41.4.438

Dammeyer, M. D., Nightingale, N. N., & McCoy, M. L. (1997). Repressed memory and other controversial origins of sexual abuse allegations: Beliefs among psychologists and clinical social workers. *Child Maltreatment, 2*(3), 252–263. doi:10.1177/1077559597002003007

Donovan, C. M. (1991). *Parenting stress in incest survivor mothers of preschool children, Vol. 51*. Ann Arbor, MI: ProQuest Information & Learning.

Dorahy, M. J., Brand, B. L., Sar, V., Kruger, K., Stavropoulos, P., Martinez-Taboas, A., . . . Middleton, W. (2014). Dissociative identity disorder:

An empirical overview. *Australian and New Zealand Journal of Psychiatry, 48*(5), 402–417.

Duncan, B. L., Miller, S. D., Wampold, B. E., & Hubble, M. A. (2010). *The heart and soul of change: Delivering what works in therapy (2nd ed.).* Washington, DC: American Psychological Association.

Duschinsky, R. (2015). The emergence of the disorganized/disoriented (D) attachment classification, 1979–1982. *History of Psychology, 18*(1), 32–46. doi:10.1037/a0038524

Egner, T., & Raz, A. (2007). Cognitive control processes and hypnosis. In G. A. Jamieson (Ed.), *Hypnosis and conscious states: The cognitive neuroscience perspective* (pp. 29–50). New York, NY: Oxford University Press.

Elhai, J. D., Miller, M. E., Ford, J. D., Biehn, T. L., Palmieri, P. A., & Frueh, B. C. (2012). Posttraumatic stress disorder in *DSM-5*: Estimates of prevalence and symptom structure in a nonclinical sample of college students. *Journal of Anxiety Disorders, 26*(1), 58–64. doi:http://dx.doi.org/10.1016/j.janxdis.2011.08.013

Elkins, G. R., Barabasz, A. F., Coucil, J. R., & Spiegel, D. (2015). Advancing research and practice: The revised APA Division 30 definition of hypnosis. *American Journal of Clinical Hypnosis, 57*, 378–385.

English, D. J., Graham, J. C., Litrownik, A. J., Everson, M., & Bangdiwala, S. I. (2005). Defining maltreatment chronicity: Are there differences in child outcomes? *Child Abuse & Neglect, 29*(5), 575–595. doi:10.1016/j.chiabu.2004.08.009

Epstein, R., Lanza, R. P., & Skinner, B. F. (1981). "Self-awareness" in the pigeon. *Science, 212*(4495), 695–696. doi:10.1126/science.212.4495.695

Erikson, E. H. (1950). *Childhood and society.* New York, NY: W. W. Norton & Co.

Erikson, E. H. (1962). *Young man Luther: A study in psychoanalysis and history.* New York, NY: W. W. Norton & Co.

Erikson, E. H. (1975). *Life history and the historical moment.* Oxford, England: W. W. Norton.

Erikson, E. H. (1980). *Identity and the life cycle.* New York, NY: W. W. Norton & Co.

Eysenck, H. J. (1952). The effects of psychotherapy. *Quarterly Bulletin of the British Psychological Society*, *3*, 41.

Felitti, V. J., Anda, R. F., Nordenberg, D., Williamson, D. F., Spitz, A. M., Edwards, V., . . . Marks, J. S. (1998). Relationship of childhood abuse and household dysfunction to many of the leading causes of death in adults: The Adverse Childhood Experiences (ACE) Study. *American Journal of Preventive Medicine*, *14*(4), 245–258. http://dx.doi.org/10.1016/S0749-3797(98)00017-8

Ferster, C. B., & Skinner, B. F. (1957a). *Schedules of reinforcement*. East Norwalk, CT: Appleton-Century-Crofts.

Ferster, C. B., & Skinner, B. F. (1957b). Variable ratio. In C. B. Ferster & B. F. Skinner (Eds.), *Schedules of reinforcement* (pp. 396–419). East Norwalk, CT: Appleton-Century-Crofts. http://dx.doi.org/10.1037/10627-007

Figueroa, E., & Silk, K. R. (1997). Biological implications of childhood sexual abuse in borderline personality disorder. *Journal of Personality Disorders*, *11*(1), 71–92. http://dx.doi.org/:10.1521/pedi.1997.11.1.71

Finkelhor, D., Ormrod, R. K., & Turner, H. A. (2007). Poly-victimization: A neglected component in child victimization. *Child Abuse & Neglect*, *31*(1), 7–26. doi:10.1016/j.chiabu.2006.06.008

Finkelhor, D., Ormrod, R. K., Turner, H. A., & Hamby, S. L. (2005). Measuring poly-victimization using the Juvenile Victimization Questionnaire. *Child Abuse & Neglect*, *29*(11), 1297–1312. doi:10.1016/j.chiabu.2005.06.005

Finkelhor, D., Turner, H., Shattuck, A., & Hamby, S. (2015). Prevalence of childhood dexposure to violence, crime, and abuse: Results from the national survey of children's exposure to violence. *JAMA:Pediatrics*, 746–754. Published online June, 29, 2015.

Foa, E. B., Keane, T. M., Friedman, M. J., Cohen, J. A. (2009). *Effective treatments for PTSD: Practice guidelines from the international society for traumatic stress studies (2nd ed.)*. New York, NY: Guilford Press.

Ford, J. D., Elhai, J. D., Connor, D. F., & Frueh, B. C. (2010). Poly-victimization and risk of posttraumatic, depressive, and substance use disorders and involvement in delinquency in a national sample of adolescents. *Journal of Adolescent Health, 46*(6), 545–552. doi:10.1016/j.jadohealth.2009.11.212

Ford, J. D., Grasso, D. J., Hawke, J., & Chapman, J. F. (2013). Poly-victimization among juvenile justice-involved youths. *Child Abuse & Neglect, 37*(10), 788–800. doi:10.1016/j.chiabu.2013.01.005

Fosha, D. (2010). Healing attachment trauma with attachment (. . .and then some!). In M. Kerman (Ed.), *Clinical pearls of wisdom: Twenty one leading therapists offer their key insights* (pp. 43–56). New York, NY: W. W. Norton & Co.

Frankl, V. E. (1997). *Man's search for meaning.* New York, NY: Pocket Books.

Frewen, P., & Lanius, R. (2015). *Healing the traumatized self: Consciousness, neuroscience, treatment.* New York: W.W. Norton & Company.

Freyd, J. J. (1996). *Betrayal trauma: The logic of forgetting childhood abuse.* Cambridge, MA: Harvard University Press.

Freyd, J. J., & Birrell, P. (2013). *Blind to betrayal: Why we fool ourseves we aren't being fooled.* Hoboken, NJ: Wiley.

Gelso, C. J. (2009a). The real relationship in a postmodern world: Theoretical and empirical explorations. *Psychotherapy Research, 19*(3), 253–264. doi:10.1080/10503300802389242

Gelso, C. J. (2009b). The time has come: The real relationship in psychotherapy research. *Psychotherapy Research, 19*(3), 278–282. doi:10.1080/10503300902777155

Guntrip, H. (1973). *Psychoanalytic theory, therapy, and the self.* New York, NY: Basic Books.

Hamby, S., Finkelhor, D., Turner, H., & Ormrod, R. (2010). The overlap of witnessing partner violence with child maltreatment and other victimizations in a nationally representative survey of youth. *Child Abuse & Neglect, 34*(10), 734–741. doi:10.1016/j.chiabu.2010.03.001

Harlow, H. F. (1997). The nature of love (1958). In J. M. Notterman (Ed.), *The evolution of psychology: Fifty years of the American Psychologist* (pp. 41–64). Washington, DC: American Psychological Association. http://dx.doi.org/10.1037/10254-004

Harlow, H. F. (2008). The monkey as a psychological subject. *Integrative Psychological & Behavioral Science, 42*(4), 336–347. doi:10.1007/s12124-008-9058-7

Harlow, H. F., & Zimmermann, R. R. (1996). Affectional responses in the infant monkey. In L. D. Houck & L. C. Drickamer (Eds.), *Foundations of animal behavior: Classic papers with commentaries* (pp. 376–387). Chicago, IL: University of Chicago Press.

Hart, O. van der, Nijenhuis, E. R. S., & Solomon, R. (2010). Dissociation of the personality in complex trauma-related disorders and EMDR: Theoretical considerations. *Journal of EMDR Practice and Research, 4*(2), 76–92. doi:10.1891/1933-3196.4.2.76

Hembree, E. A., & Foa, E. B. (2010). Cognitive behavioral treatments for PTSD. In G. M. Rosen & B. Frueh (Eds.), *Clinician's guide to posttraumatic stress disorder* (pp. 177–203). Hoboken, NJ: John Wiley & Sons Inc.

Herman, J. L. (1992). *Trauma and recovery.* New York, NY: Basic Books.

Herman, J. L. (2012). Review of special issue: Guidelines for treating dissociative identity disorder in adults (3rd revision); Rebuilding shattered lives: Treating complex PTSD and dissociative disorders; and Understanding and treating dissociative identity disorder: A relational approach. *Psychoanalytic Psychology, 29*(2), 267–269. doi:10.1037/a0027818

Herman, J. L. (2015). *Trauma and recovery: The aftermath of violence—from domestic abuse to political terror.* New York, NY: Basic Books.

Herman, J. L., & Schatzow, E. (1987). Recovery and verification of memories of childhood sexual trauma. *Psycholanalytic Psychology, 4*(1), 1–14. http://dx.doi.org/10.1037/h0079126

Herrenkohl, T. I., & Herrenkohl, R. C. (2007). Examining the overlap and prediction of multiple forms of child maltreatment, stressors, and socioeconomic status: A longitudinal analysis of youth outcomes. *Journal of Family Violence, 22*(7), 553–562. doi:10.1007/s10896-007-9107-x

Hesse, E. (1999). The adult attachment interview: Historical and current perspectives. In J. Cassidy & P. R. Shaver (Eds.), *Handbook of attachment: Theory, research, and clinical applications* (pp. 395–433). New York, NY: Guilford Press.

Higgins, D. J., & McCabe, M. P. (2001). Multiple forms of child abuse and neglect: Adult retrospective reports. *Aggression and Violent Behavior, 6*(6), 547–578. doi:10.1016/s1359-1789(00)00030-6

Holt, M. K., Finkelhor, D., & Kantor, G. K. (2007). Multiple victimization experiences of urban elementary school students: Associations with psychosocial functioning and academic performance. *Child Abuse & Neglect, 31*(5), 503–515. doi:10.1016/j.chiabu.2006.12.006

Horvath, A. O. (2013). You can't step into the same river twice, but you can stub your toes on the same rock: Psychotherapy outcome from a 50-year perspective. *Psychotherapy, 50*(1), 25–32. doi:10.1037/a0030899

Horvath, A. O., & Luborsky, L. (1993). The role of the therapeutic alliance in psychotherapy. *Journal of Consulting and Clinical Psychology, 61*(4), 561–573. doi:10.1037/0022-006X.61.4.561

Howell, E. (2011). *Understanding and treating dissociative identity disorder: A relational approach.* New York: Routledge.

Janoff-Bulman, R. (1992). *Shattered assumptions: Towards a new psychology of trauma.* New York, NY: Free Press.

Janoff-Bulman, R., & McPherson Frantz, C. (1997). The impact of trauma on meaning: From meaningless world to meaningful life. In M. J. Power & C. R. Brewin (Eds.), *The transformation of meaning in psychological therapies: Integrating theory and practice* (pp. 91–106). Hoboken, NJ: John Wiley & Sons Inc.

Janoff-Bulman, R., & Thomas, C. E. (1989). Toward an understanding of self-defeating responses following victimization. In R. Curtis (Ed.), *Self-defeating behaviors: Experimental research, clinical impressions, and practical implications* (pp. 215–234). New York, NY: Plenum Press.

Janoff-Bulman, R., & Timko, C. (1987). Coping with traumatic life events: The role of denial in light of people's assumptive worlds. In C. R. Snyder & C. E. Ford (Eds.), *Coping with negative life events: Clinical and social psychological perspectives* (pp. 135–159). New York, NY: Plenum Press.

Kierkegaard, S. (1985). *Fear and trembling* (A. Hannay, Trans.). London: Penguin.

Kinsler, P. (1992). The centrality of relationship: What's not being said. *Dissociation: Progress in the Dissociative Disorders, 5*(3), 166–170.

Kinsler, P. (2015). *Six Relational Crises.* Paper presented at the ISSTD International Conference, Orlando, FL.

Kinsler, P. (2016). From the holocaust to the treatment room: A personal journey. In R. Gartner (Ed.), *Trauma and countertrauma, resilience and counterresilience: Insights from psychoanalysts and trauma experts* (pp. 137–149). New York, NY: Routledge.

Kinsler, P., Turkus, J., & Steele, K. (2015). *Words Matter: Experts share the art of wordsmithing in therapy.* Paper presented at the International Society for the Study of Trauma and Dissociation, Orlando, FL.

Kinsler, P. J. (1995). A story for Marcie. *Dissociation: Progress in the Dissociative Disorders, 8*(2), 100–103.

Kinsler, P. J. (2014). Relationships redux: Evidence-based relationships. *Journal of Trauma & Dissociation, 15*(1), 1–5. doi:10.1080/1529973 .2013.852420

Kinsler, P. J., Courtois, C. A., & Frankel, A. S. (2009). Therapeutic alliance and risk management. In C. A. Courtois & J. D. Ford (Eds.), *Treating complex traumatic stress disorders: An evidence-based guide* (pp. 183–201). New York, NY: Guilford Press.

Kinsler, P. J., & Saxman, A. (2007). Traumatized offenders: Don't look now, but your jail's also your mental health center. *Journal of Trauma & Dissociation, 8*(2), 81–95. doi:10.1300/J229v08n02_06

Kluft, R. P. (1984). Treatment of multiple personality disorder: A study of 33 cases. *Psychiatric Clinics of North America, 7*(1), 9–29.

Kluft, R. P. (1985). Hypnotherapy of childhood multiple personality disorder. *American Journal of Clinical Hypnosis, 27*(4), 201–210.

Kluft, R. P. (1986). Preliminary observations on age regression in multiple personality disorder patients before and after integration. *American Journal of Clinical Hypnosis, 28*(3), 147–156.

Kluft, R. P. (1993a). Basic principles in conducting the psychotherapy of multiple personality disorder. In R. P. Kluft, & C. G. Fine (Eds.), *Clinical perspectives on multiple personality disorder* (pp. 19–50). Arlington, VA: American Psychiatric Association.

Kluft, R. P. (1993b). Clinical perspectives on multiple personality disorder. In R. P. Kluft & C. G. Fine (Eds.), *Clinical perspectives on multiple personality disorder.* Arlington, VA: American Psychiatric Association.

Kluft, R. P. (1993c). The initial stages of psychotherapy in the treatment of multiple personality disorder patients. *Dissociation: Progress in the Dissociative Disorders, 6*(2–3), 145–161.

Kluft, R. P. (1993d). The treatment of dissociative disorder patients: An overview of discoveries, successes, and failures. *Dissociation: Progress in the Dissociative Disorders*, 6(2–3), 87–101.

Kluft, R. P. (1994). Treatment trajectories in multiple personality disorder. *Dissociation: Progress in the Dissociative Disorders*, 7(1), 63–76.

Kluft, R. P. (2006). Dealing with alters: A pragmatic clinical perspective. *Psychiatric Clinics of North America*, 29(1), 281–304. doi:10.1016/j.psc.2005.10.010

Kluft, R. P. (2012a). Hypnosis in the treatment of dissociative identity disorder and allied state: An overview and case study. *South African Journal of Psychology*, 42(2), 146–155. doi:10.1177/008124631204200202

Kluft, R. P. (2012b). The same old elephant. . . *Journal of Trauma & Dissociation*, 13(3), 259–270. doi:10.1080/15299732.2011.652347

Kluft, R. P. (2015). The revised APA Division 30 definition of hypnosis: An appreciation, a commentary, and a wish list. *American Journal of Clinical Hypnosis*, 57(4), 431–438. doi:10.1080/00029157.2015.1011495

Kluft, R. P., Kinsler, P. J., & O'Neil, J. (2014). *What Does Heinz Kohut Have to Teach Us About Dissociation?* Paper presented at the International Society for the Study of Trauma and Dissociation, Long Beach, CA.

Kohut, H. (1977). *The restoration of the self.* Chicago, IL: University of Chicago Press.

Kohut, H., & Wolf, E. S. (1992). The disorders of the self and their treatment. In D. Capps & R. K. Fenn (Eds.), *Individualism reconsidered: Readings bearing on the endangered self in modern society* (pp. 315–327). Princeton, NJ: Princeton Theological Seminary.

Kolk, B. A. van der, (1996). The body keeps score: Approaches to the psychobiology of posttraumatic stress disorder. In B. A. van der Kolk & A. C. McFarlane (Eds.), *Traumatic stress: The effects of overwhelming experience on mind, body, and society* (pp. 214–241). New York, NY: Guilford Press.

Kolk, B. A. van der, (2002). Posttraumatic therapy in the age of neuroscience. *Psychoanalytic Dialogues*, 12(3), 381–392. doi:10.1080/10481881209348674

Kolk, B. A. van der, (2004). Psychobiology of posttraumatic stress disorder. In B. A. van der Kolk & J. Panksepp (Eds.), *Textbook of biological psychiatry* (pp. 319–344). New York, NY: Wiley-Liss.

Kolk, B. A. van der, (2005). Developmental trauma disorder: Toward a rational diagnosis for children with complex trauma histories. *Psychiatric Annals, 35*(5), 401–408.

Kolk, B. A. van der, (2007). The developmental impact of childhood trauma. In L. J. Kimayer, R. Lemelson, & M. Barad (Eds.), *Understanding trauma: Integrating biological, clinical, and cultural perspectives* (pp. 224–241). New York, NY: Cambridge University Press. http://dx.doi.org/10.1017/CBO9780511500008.016

Kolk, B. A. van der, (2014). *The body keeps the score: Brain, mind, and body in the healing of trauma.* New York, NY: Viking.

Landry, M., & Raz, A. (2015). Hypnosis and imaging of the living human brain. *American Journal of Clinical Hypnosis, 57*(3), 285–313. doi:10.1080/00029157.2014.978496

Langs, R. (1980). Truth therapy/lie therapy. *International Journal of Psychoanalytic Psychotherapy, 8,* 3–34.

Langs, R. (1984). Making interpretations and securing the frame: Sources of danger for psychotherapists. *International Journal of Psychoanalytic Psychotherapy, 10,* 3–23.

Langs, R. (1992). Boundaries & frames: Non-transference in teaching. *International Journal of Communicative Psychoanalysis & Psychotherapy, 7*(3–4), 125–130.

Langs, R. (2004). *The power of ground rules.* Mahwah, NJ: Lawrence Erlbaum Associates Publishers.

Lanius, R., Vermetten, E., Loewenstein, R., Brand, B., Schmahl, C., Bremner, J. D., & Spiegel, D. (2010). Emotion modulation in PTSD: Clinical and neurobiological evidence for a dissociative subtype. *American Journal of Psychiatry, 167*(6, June), 640–647.

Lanius, R. A., Wolf, E. J., Miller, M. W., Frewen, P. A., Vermetten, E., Brand, B., & Spiegel, D. (2014). The dissociative subtype of PTSD. In M. J. Friedman, T. M. Keane, & P. A. Resick (Eds.), *Handbook of PTSD: Science and practice (2nd ed.)* (pp. 234–250). New York, NY: Guilford Press.

Lazarus, R. S. (1984). On the primacy of cognition. *American Psychologist, 39*(2), 124–129. doi:10.1037/0003-066X.39.2.124

Levin, R., Bachner-Melman, R., Edelman, S., Ebstein, R. P., Heresco-Levy, U., & Lichtenberg, P. (2013). Hypnotizability is associated with a protective but not acquisitive self-presentation style. *International Journal of Clinical and Experimental Hypnosis, 61*(2), 183–192. doi:10.1080/00207144.2013.753830

Lichtenberg, P., Even-Or, E., Bar, G., Levin, R., Brin, A., & Heresco-Levy, U. (2008). Reduced prepulse inhibition is associated with increased hypnotizability. *International Journal of Neuropsychopharmacology, 11*(4), 541–545. doi:10.1017/S1461145707008231

Lifshitz, M., Campbell, N. K. J., & Raz, A. (2012). Varieties of attention in hypnosis and meditation. *Consciousness and Cognition: An International Journal, 21*(3), 1582–1585. doi:10.1016/j.concog.2012.05.008

Loftus, E. F. (2003). The dangers of memory. In R. J. Sternberg (Ed.), *Psychologists defying the crowd: Stories of those who battled the establishment and won* (pp. 105–117). Washington, DC: American Psychological Association. http://dx.doi.org/10.1037/10483-007

Main, M. (1995). Recent studies in attachment: Overview, with selected implications for clinical work. In S. Goldberg, R. Muir, & J. Kerr (Eds.), *Attachment theory: Social, developmental, and clinical perspectives* (pp. 407–474). Hillsdale, NJ: Analytic Press, Inc.

Main, M. (2000). Attachment theory. In A. E. Kazdin (Ed.), *Encyclopedia of psychology, Vol. 1* (pp. 289–293). New York, NY: Oxford University Press. http://dx.doi.org/10.1037/10516-102

Main, M., Hesse, E., & Kaplan, N. (2005). Predictability of attachment behavior and representational processes at 1, 6, and 19 Years of Age: The Berkeley longitudinal study. In K. E. Grossmann, K. Grossmann, & E. Waters (Eds.), *Attachment from infancy to adulthood: The major longitudinal studies* (pp. 245–304). New York, NY: Guilford Publications.

Main, M., Kaplan, N., & Cassidy, J. (1985). Security in infancy, childhood, and adulthood: A move to the level of representation. *Monographs of the Society for Research in Child Development, 50*(1–2), 66–104. doi:10.2307/3333827

McLean, C. P., Asnaani, A., & Foa, E. B. (2015). Prolonged exposure therapy. In U. Schnyder & M. Cloitre (Eds.), *Evidence based treatments for trauma-related psychological disorders: A practical guide for clinicians* (pp. 143–159). Cham, Switzerland: Springer International Publishing.

McNally, R. J. (2003). Experimental approaches to the recovered memory controversy. In M. F. Lenzenweger & J. M. Hooley (Eds.), *Principles of experimental psychopathology: Essays in honor of Brendan A. Maher* (pp. 269–277). Washington, DC: American Psychological Association. http://dx.doi.org/10,1037/10477-017

Meyer, J. S., Novak, M. A., Bowman, R. E., & Harlow, H. F. (1975). Behavioral and hormonal effects of attachment object separation in surrogate-peer-reared and mother-reared infant rhesus monkeys. *Developmental Psychobiology, 8*(5), 425–435. doi:10.1002/dev.420080507

Mickleborough, M. J. S., Daniels, J. K., Coupland, N. J., Kao, R., Williamson, P. C., Lanius, U. F., . . . Lanius, R. A. (2011). Effects of trauma-related cues on pain processing in posttraumatic stress disorder: An fMRI investigation. *Journal of Psychiatry & Neuroscience, 36*(1), 6–14. doi:10.1503/jpn.080188

Nathanson, D. L. (1987). The shame/pride axis. In H. B. Lewis (Ed.), *The role of shame in symptom formation* (pp. 183–205). Hillsdale, NJ: Lawrence Erlbaum Associates, Inc.

Nathanson, D. L. (1997a). Affect theory and the compass of shame. In M. R. Lansky & A. P. Morrison (Eds.), *The widening scope of shame* (pp. 339–354). Mahwah, NJ: Analytic Press.

Nathanson, D. L. (1997b). Shame and the affect theory of Silvan Tomkins. In M. R. Lansky & A. P. Morrison (Eds.), *The widening scope of shame* (pp. 107–138). Mahwah, NJ: Analytic Press.

Nayak, N., Powers, M. B., & Foa, E. B. (2012). Empirically supported psychological treatments: Prolonged exposure. In J. G. Beck & D. M. Sloan (Eds.), *The Oxford handbook of traumatic stress disorders* (pp. 427–438). New York, NY: Oxford University Press.

Norcross, J. C., & Wampold, B. E. (2011). Evidence-based therapy relationships: Research conclusions and clinical practices. *Psychotherapy, 48*(1), 98–102. doi:10.1037/a0022161

Ornstein, P. A., Ceci, S. J., & Loftus, E. F. (1998a). Comment on Alpert, Brown, and Courtois (1998). The science of memory and the practice of psychotherapy. *Psychology, Public Policy, and Law, 4*(4), 996–1010. doi:10.1037/1076-8971.4.4.996

Ornstein, P. A., Ceci, S. J., & Loftus, E. F. (1998b). More on the repressed memory debate: A reply to Alpert, Brown, and Courtois (1998). *Psychology, Public Policy, and Law, 4*(4), 1068–1078. doi:10.1037/1076-8971.4.4.1068

Pearlman, L. A. (1997). Trauma and the self: A theoretical and clinical perspective. *Journal of Emotional Abuse, 1*(1), 7–25. doi:10.1300/J135v01n01_02

Pearlman, L. A., & Courtois, C. A. (2005). Clinical applications of the attachment framework: Relational treatment of complex trauma. *Journal of Traumatic Stress, 18*(5), 449–459. doi:10.1002/jts.20052

Pfister, O. (1917). The practical benefits. In O. P. Pfister & C. Rockwell (Eds. and Trans.), *The psychoanalytic method* (pp. 535–543). New York, NY: Moffat, Yard & Company. http//dx.doi.org/10.1037/13862-025

Pope, K. S., & Brown, L. S. (1996a). Clinical and forensic work as questioning: Considering claims about false memories. In K. S. Pope & L. S. Brown (Eds.), *Recovered memories of abuse: Assessment, therapy, forensics* (pp. 67–107). Washington, DC: American Psychological Association. http://dx.doi.org/10.1037/10214-003

Pope, K. S., & Brown, L. S. (1996b). Clinical work with people who report recovered memories. In K. S. Pope & L. S. Brown (Eds.), *Recovered memories of abuse: Assessment, therapy, forensics* (pp. 145–205). Washington, DC: American Psychological Association. http://dx.doi.org/10.1037/10214-005

Pope, K. S., & Brown, L. S. (1996c). Science, memory, and trauma: A brief overview. In K. S. Pope & L. S. Brown (Eds.), *Recovered memories of abuse: Assessment, therapy, forensics* (pp. 23–65). Washington, DC: American Psychological Association. http://dx.doi.org/10.1037/10214-002

Pope, K. S., Sonne, J., & Holroyd, J. (1993). *Sexual feelings in psychotheraoy: Explorations for therapists and therapists-in-training.* Washington, DC: American Psychological Association.

Porges, S. W. (1998). Love: An emergent property of the mammalian autonomic nervous system [Press release]. Retrieved from www.psyneuen-journal.com/article/S0306-4530(98)00057-2/abstract

Porges, S. W. (2001). The polyvagal theory: Phylogenetic substrates of a social nervous system. *International Journal of Psychophysiology*, *42*(2), 123–146. doi:10.1016/S0167-8760(01)00162-3

Porges, S. W. (2003a). The polyvagal theory: Phylogenetic contributions to social behavior. *Physiology & Behavior*, *79*(3), 503–513. doi:10.1016/S0031-9384(03)00156-2

Porges, S. W. (2003b). Social engagement and attachment: A Phylogenetic Perspective. In J. A. King, C. F. Ferris, & I. I. Lederhendler (Eds.), *Roots of mental illness in children* (pp. 31–47). New York, NY: New York Academy of Sciences.

Porges, S. W. (2005). The role of social engagement in attachment and bonding: A phylogenetic perspective. In C. S. Carter, L. Ahnert, K. E. Grossmann, S. B. Hrdy, M. E. Lamb, S. W. Porges, & N. Sachser (Eds.), *Attachment and bonding: A new synthesis* (pp. 33–54). Cambridge, MA: MIT Press.

Porges, S. W. (2009). Reciprocal influences between body and brain in the perception and expression of affect: A polyvagal perspective. In D. Fosha, D. J. Siegel, & M. F. Solomon (Eds.), *The healing power of emotion: Affective neuroscience, development & clinical practice* (pp. 27–54). New York, NY: W. W. Norton & Co.

Porges, S. W. (2011). *The polyvagal theory: Neurophysiological foundations of emotions, attachment, communication, and self-regulation.* New York, NY: W. W. Norton & Co.

Porges, S. W., & Furman, S. A. (2011). The early development of the autonomic nervous system provides a neural platform for social behaviour: A polyvagal perspective. *Infant and Child Development*, *20*(1), 106–118. doi:10.1002/icd.688

Rachman, S. (1981). The primacy of affect: Some theoretical implications. *Behaviour Research and Therapy*, *19*(4), 279–290. doi:10.1016/0005-7967(81)90048-6

Raskin, N. J., & Rogers, C. R. (2005). Person-centered therapy. In D. Wedding (Ed.), *Current psychotherapies (7th ed., instr. ed.)* (pp. 130–165). Belmont, CA: Thomson Brooks/Cole Publishing Co.

Raz, A. (2005). Attention and hypnosis: Neural substrates and genetic associations of two converging processes. *International Journal of Clinical and Experimental Hypnosis*, *53*(3), 237–258. doi:10.1080/00207140590961295

Raz, A. (2007). Suggestibility and hypnotizability: Mind the gap. *American Journal of Clinical Hypnosis, 49*(3), 205–210. doi:10.1080/00029157.2007.10401582

Raz, A. (2011). Hypnosis: A twilight zone of the top-down variety: Few have never heard of hypnosis but most know little about the potential of this mind–body regulation technique for advancing science. *Trends in Cognitive Sciences, 15*(12), 555–557. doi:10.1016/j.tics.2011.10.002

Raz, A. (2012). Hypnosis as a lens to the development of attention. *Consciousness and Cognition: An International Journal, 21*(3), 1595–1598. doi:10.1016/j.concog.2012.05.011

Raz, A., Fan, J., & Posner, M. I. (2005). Hypnotic suggestion reduces conflict in the human brain. *PNAS Proceedings of the National Academy of Sciences of the United States of America, 102*(28), 9978–9983. doi:10.1073/pnas.0503064102

Renner, L. M., & Slack, K. S. (2006). Intimate partner violence and child maltreatment: Understanding intra- and intergenerational connections. *Child Abuse & Neglect, 30*(6), 599–617. doi:10.1016/j.chiabu.2005.12.005

Rogers, C. R. (1975). Empathic: An unappreciated way of being. *The Counseling Psychologist, 5*(2), 2–10. doi:10.1177/001100007500500202

Rogers, C. R. (2007a). The basic conditions of the facilitative therapeutic relationship. In M. Cooper, M. O. Hara, P. F. Schmid, & G. Wyatt (Eds.), *The handbook of person-centred psychotherapy and counselling* (pp. 1–5). New York, NY: Palgrave Macmillan.

Rogers, C. R. (2007b). The necessary and sufficient conditions of therapeutic personality change. *Psychotherapy: Theory, Research, Practice, Training, 44*(3), 240–248. doi:10.1037/0033-3204.44.3.240

Schore, A. N. (1991). Early superego development: The emergence of shame and narcissistic affect regulation in the practicing period. *Psychoanalysis & Contemporary Thought, 14*(2), 187–250.

Schore, A. N. (1994). *Affect regulation and the origin of the self: The neurobiology of emotional development.* Hillsdale, NJ, England: Lawrence Erlbaum Associates, Inc.

Schore, A. N. (1996). The experience-dependent maturation of a regulatory system in the orbital prefrontal cortex and the origin of developmental psychopathology. *Development and Psychopathology, 8*(1), 59–87. doi:10.1017/s0954579400006970

Schore, A. N. (1997). Early organization of the nonlinear right brain and development of a predisposition to psychiatric disorders. *Development and Psychopathology, 9*(4), 595–631. doi:10.1017/s0954579497001363

Schore, A. N. (1998a). Early shame experiences and infant brain development. In P. Gilbert & B. Andrews (Eds.), *Shame: Interpersonal behavior, psychopathology, and culture* (pp. 57–77). New York, NY: Oxford University Press.

Schore, A. N. (1998b). The experience-dependent maturation of an evaluative system in the cortex. In K. H. Pribram (Ed.), *Brain and values: Is a biological science of values possible?* (pp. 337–358). Mahwah, NJ: Lawrence Erlbaum Associates Publishers.

Schore, A. N. (2000a). Attachment and the regulation of the right brain. *Attachment & Human Development, 2*(1), 23–47. doi:10.1080/146167300361309

Schore, A. N. (2000b). The self-organization of the right brain and the neurobiology of emotional development. In M. D. Lewis & I. Granic (Eds.), *Emotion, development, and self-organization: Dynamic systems approaches to emotional development* (pp. 155–185). New York, NY: Cambridge University Press. http://dx.doi.org/10.1017/CBO9780511527883.008

Schore, A. N. (2001a). Effects of a secure attachment relationship on right brain development, affect regulation, and infant mental health. *Infant Mental Health Journal, 22*(1–2), 7–66. doi:10.1002/10970355(200101/04)22:1<7::aid-imhj2>3.0.co;2-n

Schore, A. N. (2001b). The effects of early relational trauma on right brain development, affect regulation, and infant mental health. *Infant Mental Health Journal, 22*(1–2), 201–269. doi:10.1002/1097-0355(200101/04)22:1<201::aid-imhj8>3.0.co;2-9

Schore, A. N. (2002a). Dysregulation of the right brain: A fundamental mechanism of traumatic attachment and the psychopathogenesis of posttraumatic stress disorder. *Australian and New Zealand Journal of Psychiatry, 36*(1), 9–30. doi:10.1046/j.1440-1614.2002.00996.x

Schore, A. N. (2002b). The neurobiology of attachment and early personality organization. *Journal of Prenatal & Perinatal Psychology & Health, 16*(3), 249–263.

Schore, A. N. (2003a). *Affect dysregulation and disorders of the self.* New York, NY: W. W. Norton & Co.

Schore, A. N. (2003b). *Affect regulation and the repair of the self.* New York, NY: W. W. Norton & Co.

Schore, A. N. (2009a). Attachment trauma and the developing right brain: Origins of pathological dissociation. In P.F. Dell & J. A. O'Neil (Eds.), *Dissociation and the dissociative disorders: DSM-V and beyond* (pp. 107–141). New York, NY: Routledge/Taylor & Francis Group.

Schore, A. N. (2009b). Relational trauma and the developing right brain: An interface of psychoanalytic self psychology and neuroscience. In W. J. Coburn & N. Van Der Heide (Eds.), *Self and systems: Explorations in contemporary self psychology* (pp. 189–203). Wiley-Blackwell.

Schore, A. N. (2010). Relational trauma and the developing right brain: The neurobiology of broken attachment bonds. In T. Baradon (Ed.), *Relational trauma in infancy: Psychoanalytic, attachment and neuropsychological contributions to parent—infant psychotherapy* (pp. 19–47). New York, NY: Routledge/Taylor & Francis Group.

Schore, A. N. (2011). The right brain implicit self lies at the core of psychoanalysis. *Psychoanalytic Dialogues, 21*(1), 75–100. doi:10.1080/10481885.2011.545329

Schore, A. N. (2012). *The science of the art of psychotherapy.* New York, New York: WW Norton.

Schore, A. N., & McIntosh, J. (2011). Family law and the neuroscience of attachment, part I. *Family Court Review, 49*(3), 501–512. doi:10.1111/j.1744-1617.2011.01387.x

Schore, J. R., & Schore, A. N. (2008). Modern attachment theory: The central role of affect regulation in development and treatment. *Clinical Social Work Journal, 36*(1), 9–20. doi:10.1007/s10615-007-0111-7

Shapiro, F. (2001). *Eye movement desensitization and reprocessing: Basic principles, protocols, and procedures new.* New York, NY: Guiiford Press.

Siegel, D. J. (1999). *The developing mind: Toward a neurobiology of inter-personal experience.* New York, NY: Guilford Press.

Siegel, D. J. (2001). Toward an interpersonal neurobiology of the developing mind: Attachment relationships, "mindsight", and neural integration. *Infant Mental Health Journal, 22*(1–2), 67–94. doi:10.1002/1097-0355 (200101/04)22:1<67::AID-IMHJ3>3.0.CO;2-G

Siegel, D. J. (2002). The developing mind and the resolution of trauma: Some ideas about information processing and an interpersonal neu-robiology of psychotherapy. In F. Shapiro (Ed.), *EMDR as an inte-grative psychotherapy approach: Experts of diverse orientations explore the paradigm prism* (pp. 85–121). Washington, DC: American Psy-chological Association. http://dx.doi.org/10.1037/10512-004

Siegel, D. J. (2004). Attachment and self-understanding: Parenting with the brain in mind. *Journal of Prenatal & Perinatal Psychology & Health, 18*(4), 273–285.

Siegel, D. J. (2012a). *The developing mind: How relationships and the brain interact to shape who we are (2nd ed.).* New York, NY: Guilford Press.

Siegel, D. J. (2012b). *Pocket guide to interpersonal neurobiology: An inte-grative handbook of the mind.* New York, NY: W. W. Norton & Co.

Silverstein, S. (1976). *The missing piece.* New York: HarperCollins.

Skinner, B. F. (1992). "Superstition" in the pigeon. *Journal of Experimen-tal Psychology: General, 121*(3), 273–274. doi:10.1037/0096-3445 .121.3.273

Smith, D. W., McCart, M. R., & Saunders, B. E. (2008). PTSD in chil-dren and adolescents: Risk factors and treatment innovations. In D. W. Smith, M. R. McCart, & B. E. Saunders (Eds.), *The psychobiology of trauma and resilience across the lifespan* (pp. 69–88). Lanham, MD: Jason Aronson.

Smith, M. L., & Glass, G. V. (1977). Meta-analysis of psychotherapy outcome studies. *American Psychologist, 32*(9), 752–760. doi:10.1037/ 0003-066X.32.9.752

Spanos, N. P. (1996a). *Multiple identities & false memories: A sociocognitive perspective.* Washington, DC: American Psychological Association.

Spanos, N. P. (1996b). Multiple personality disorder, recovered memo-ries, and sociopolitical considerations. In N. P. Spanos (Ed.), *Multiple identities and false memories: A sociocognitive perspective* (pp. 287–298).

Washington, DC: American Psychological Association. http://
dx.doi.org/10.1037/10216-020

Spanos, N. P. (1996c). UFO abduction: An example of complex false
memory. In N. P. Spanos (Ed.), *Multiple identities and false memories: A
sociocognitive perspective* (pp. 117–129). Washington, DC: American
Psychological Association. http://dx.doi.org/10.1037/10216-009

Spinazzola, J., Ford, J. D., Zucker, M., van der Kolk, B. A., Silva, S.,
Smith, S. F., & Blaustein, M. (2005). Survey evaluates complex
trauma exposure, outcome, and intervention among children and
adolescents. *Psychiatric Annals, 35*(5), 433–439.

Steele, K. (1989). Sitting with the shattered soul. *Pilgrimage: Journal of
Psychotherapy and Personal Exploration, 15*(6), 19–25.

Strathearn, L. (2007). Exploring the neurobiology of attachment. In
L. Mayes, P. Fonagy, & M. Target (Eds.), *Developmental science and
psychoanalysis: Integration and innovation* (pp. 117–140). London,
England: Karnac Books.

Strupp, H. H. (1962). Psychotherapy. *Annual Review of Psychology, 13*,
445–478. doi:10.1146/annurev.ps.13.020162.002305

Strupp, H. H. (1963). The outcome problem in psychotherapy revisited.
Psychotherapy: Theory, Research & Practice, 1(1), 1–13. doi:10.1037
/h0088565

Strupp, H. H. (1964). The outcome problem in psychotherapy: A rejoin-
der. *Psychotherapy: Theory, Research & Practice, 1*(3), 101. doi:10.1037
/h0088579

Strupp, H. H. (1967). Who needs intrapsychic factors in clinical psychology? *Psychotherapy: Theory, Research & Practice, 4*(4), 145–150.
doi:10.1037/h0087955

Strupp, H. H. (1970). Specific vs. nonspecific factors in psychotherapy
and the problem of control. *Archives of General Psychiatry, 23*(5),
393–401. doi:10.1001/archpsyc.1970.01750050009002

Strupp, H. H. (1971). Client-centered psychotherapy. In H. H. Strupp
(Ed.), *Psychotherapy and the modification of abnormal behavior: An intro-
duction to theory and research* (pp. 37–50). New York, NY: McGraw-
Hill Book Company. http://dx.doi.org/10.1037/11524-003

Strupp, H. H. (1972). Needed: A reformulation of the psychotherapeu-
tic influence. *International Journal of Psychiatry, 10*(2), 114–120.

Strupp, H. H. (1973a). On the basic ingredients of psychotherapy. *Journal of Consulting and Clinical Psychology*, *41*(1), 1–8. doi:10.1037/h0035619

Strupp, H. H. (1973b). The therapist: Personal and technical factors. In H. H. Strupp (Ed.), *Psychotherapy: Clinical, research, and theoretical issues* (pp. 27–54). Lanham, MD: Jason Aronson. http://dx.doi.org/10.1037/11523-001

Sullivan, H. S. (1938). Psychiatry: Introduction to the study of interpersonal relations. *Psychiatry: Journal for the Study of Interpersonal Processes*, *1*, 121–134.

Suomi, S. J., & Harlow, H. F. (1977). Depression: Production and alleviation of depressive behaviors in monkeys. In J. D. Maser & E. P. Martin (Eds.), *Psychopathology: Experimental models* (pp. 131–173). New York, NY: W. H. Freeman/Times Books/Henry Holt and Co.

Truax, C. B., & Carkhuff, R. R. (1967). *Toward effective counseling and psychotherapy: Training and practice.* Hawthorne, NY: Aldine Publishing Co.

Tsu, L., & Gia-Fu, F. (1989). *Tao Te Ching.* New York, NY: Vintage.

Turkus, J. (2014). *Suicidality, Self-Harm, Homicidality.* Paper presented at the ISSTD International Conference, Washington, DC.

Turkus, J., & Kinsler, P. (2014). *Don't tear your hair out: We can manage suicidality, homicidality, and self-injurious behaviors.* Paper presented at the International Society for the Study of Trauma and Dissociation, Long Beach, CA.

Turner, H. A., Finkelhor, D., Hamby, S. L., & Shattuck, A. (2013). Family structure, victimization, and child mental health in a nationally representative sample. *Social Science & Medicine*, *87*, 39–51. doi:10.1016/j.socscimed.2013.02.034

Turner, H. A., Finkelhor, D., & Ormrod, R. (2010). Poly-victimization in a national sample of children and youth. *American Journal of Preventive Medicine*, *38*(3), 323–330. doi:10.1016/j.amepre.2009.11.012

Van Bertalanffy, L. (1952). Theoretical models in biology and psychology. In D. Krech (Ed.), *Theoretical models and personality theory* (pp. 24–38). Durham, NC: Duke University Press.

White, R. W. (1959). Motivation reconsidered: The concept of competence. *Psychological Review*, *66*(5), 297–333. doi:10.1037/h0040934

Wikipedia. (2016). Principles of Grouping. Retrieved from https://en.wikipedia.org/wiki/Principles_of_grouping

Wilson, J. P., & Lindy, J. D. (1994). Empathic strain and countertransference. In J. P. Wilson & J. D. Lindy (Eds.), *Countertransference in the treatment of PTSD* (pp. 5–30). New York, NY: Guilford Press.

Winnicott, D. W. (1957a). *The child and his family: First relationships. [The child and his family: First relationships].* Oxford, England: Petite Bibliotheque Payot.

Winnicott, D. W. (1957b). *Mother and child: A primer of first relationships.* Oxford, England: Basic Books.

Winnicott, D. W. (1958). The capacity to be alone. *The International Journal of Psychoanalysis, 39,* 416–420.

Winnicott, D. W. (1965). *The maturational processes and the facilitating environment: Studies in the theory of emotional development.* Oxford, England: International Universities Press.

Winnicott, D. W. (1969). *The child, the family, and the outside world.* Oxford, England: Penguin Books.

Wolpe, J. (1959). Psychotherapy based on the principle of reciprocal inhibition. In A. Burton (Ed.), *Case studies in counseling and psychotherapy* (pp. 353–381). Englewood Cliffs, NJ: Prentice-Hall, Inc. http://dx.doi.org/10.1037/10575-013

Wolpe, J. (1968). Psychotherapy by reciprocal inhibition. *Conditional Reflex, 3*(4), 234–240.

Wolpe, J. (1969). *The practice of behavior therapy.* Oxford, England: Pergamon.

Wolpe, J., & Lazarus, A. A. (1966). *Behavior therapy techniques: A guide to the treatment of neuroses.* Elmsford, NY: Pergamon Press.

Wouk, H. (1993). *The hope: A novel.* New York, NY: Little, Brown & Company.

Wouk, H. (1994). *The Glory.* New York, NY: Little, Brown & Company.

Zajonc, R. B. (1984). On the primacy of affect. *American Psychologist, 39*(2), 117–123. doi:10.1037/0003-066X.39.2.117

INDEX